2   Welcome
    Andrew Nairne

3   Foreword
    Jim Ede

6   Introduction to Kettle's Yard

14   Kettle's Yard Today
     Jennifer Powell

Cottages

16   Sitting and Dining Room

22   Bedroom and Bathroom

28   Bechstein Room

34   Helen's Bedroom and Bathroom

38   Attic

42   Bridge and Dancer Room

Extension

48   Upstairs

50   Library

56   Downstairs Upper Level

62   Downstairs Lower Level

68   Biographical Notes

Welcome to the Kettle's Yard House
Andrew Nairne

Kettle's Yard is a remarkable place, created by a remarkable man. In a quiet corner of Cambridge, overlooking St Peter's Church, is a beautiful house filled with beautiful objects, once the home of H. S. (Jim) Ede and his wife, Helen. Here their collection of twentieth century British and European art is displayed alongside found and natural objects, ceramics, glass, textiles and furniture. Over 100 artists are represented in the collection, including works by Henri Gaudier-Brzeska, Joan Miró, Constantin Brancusi, Naum Gabo, Christopher Wood, Alfred Wallis, Barbara Hepworth, David Jones, Henry Moore, Ben Nicholson and Winifred Nicholson. The contents of the house and their display reflect Jim Ede's life and travels, his friendships with the pioneering artists of his time, his eye for found objects and an affinity with nature.

The Edes lived here for over fifteen years, welcoming visitors into their home every afternoon, and hosting concerts first in the tiny upstairs living room, and later in the 1970 extension designed by David Owers and Leslie Martin, one of the architects responsible for the Royal Festival Hall on London's South Bank. Also in 1970, the first of a sequence of small galleries was built for temporary exhibitions. Today, with the new galleries and an Education Wing, Kettle's Yard hosts an ambitious year round programme of exhibitions, events and activities.

The House is by and large as Jim left it, in the care of the University of Cambridge, in 1973. There are artworks in every corner, and there are no labels. A lemon still sits on the pewter plate, waiting for Jim's lesson about balance and the spot of yellow to be found in the Miró painting hanging on the opposite wall. Every day except Mondays, visitors are welcomed into the house, much as Jim would have welcomed them. He encouraged visitors to sit and spend time here, to pay as much attention to a worn broom head or the play of afternoon light as the drawings, paintings and sculptures in every room.

Today the Kettle's Yard house is widely recognised as an influential masterclass in curating; a flawless arrangement of art and objects that is still radical in its philosophy of seeking to fuse art with life. For many it is a place that has that rare power of changing how we see the world and our place within it.

Foreword
Jim Ede

I have been asked to write a personal note on how Kettle's Yard was formed. I suppose it began by my meeting with Ben and Winifred Nicholson in 1924 or thereabouts, while I was an Assistant at the Tate Gallery. It started of course before that; I was fifteen at the Leys School in Cambridge and fell in love with early Italian painting and broke bounds to search the Free Library and Fitzwilliam Museum, and before that at thirteen when I first visited the Louvre, saw nothing, but fell for Puvis de Chavannes near the little church of St Etienne du Mont.

So it wasn't until I was nearly thirty that the Nicholsons opened a door into the world of contemporary art and I rushed headlong into the arms of Picasso, Brancusi and Braque; not losing, however, my rapture over Giotto, Angelico, Monaco and Piero della Francesca.

Ben Nicholson shared this rapture and I saw in his work a simple continuity from them into the everyday world of the twenties and thirties. There was no longer a break. Oddly enough I turned out to be one of Ben Nicholson's very few admirers at that time, and after he had tried to sell a painting for a year or so he would tell me that I could have it for the price of the canvas and frame, usually one to three pounds. I could not always manage it, for my salary was under £250 a year; not much to maintain a family in London. Many he would give me, and now that Kettle's Yard has been catalogued I find it has forty-four works by him, and many others have been given away.

Winifred Nicholson taught me much about the fusing of art and daily living, and Ben Nicholson that traffic in Piccadilly had the rhythm of a ballet, and a game of tennis the perfection of an old master. Life with them at once seemed lively, satisfying and special.

Then came Kit [Christopher] Wood and David Jones. From Kit I learnt a clarity of perspective in regard to contemporary painters; a direct enjoyment, spontaneous and easy, which became a touchstone in the world of what has often been called naive painting; and so came Douanier Rousseau and with him no doubt many works now held by Kettle's Yard. David Jones was different, he brought shape to the ephemeral in me, his profound vision of essential truth supported me. He had a tolerance not usual in artists and this enlarged my vision.

I think it was in 1926 I first began to get paintings by Alfred Wallis. They would come by post, perhaps sixty at a time, and the price fixed at one, two or three shillings according to size. I once got as many as twenty but usually could not afford so many. I suppose that Kettle's Yard now has a hundred.

In that same year I first heard of Henri Gaudier-Brzeska. A great quantity of his work was dumped in my office at the Tate: it happened to be the Board Room and the only place with a large table. It was ten years after Gaudier's death and all this work had been sent to many art experts for their opinion, and London dealers had been asked to buy. It had become the property of the Treasury and the enlightened Solicitor General thought that the Nation should acquire it, but no, not even as a gift. In the end I got a friend to buy three works for the Tate and three for the Contemporary Art Society, and the rest, for a song, I bought. Since then it has seemed my task to get Gaudier established in the rightful position he would have achieved had he lived into this present time. The principal collections of his work today are the Tate Gallery, the Musée national d'art moderne in Paris and Kettle's Yard, and he will surely, in time, be recognised as one of France's greatest sculptors and probably the most vital of his epoch.

Thus we come to 1936 when, save for the period of the Second World War, I left England for twenty years, living in Morocco and France and lecturing on art all over the United States. This brought me to Richard Pousette-Dart, a passionate follower of Gaudier-Brzeska and to William Congdon whose paintings of Venice at last exorcised Sargent and brought me back to Bellini. In England there was William Scott, Roger Hilton and recently that devoted 'primitive' Bryan Pearce.

It was while we were still abroad in 1954 that I found myself first dreaming of the idea of somehow creating a living place where works of art could be enjoyed, inherent to the domestic setting, where young people could be at home unhampered by the greater austerity of the museum or public art gallery and where an informality might infuse an underlying formality. I wanted, in a modest way, to use the inspiration I had had from beautiful interiors, houses of leisured elegance, and to combine it with the joy I had felt in individual works seen in museums and with the all embracing delight I had experienced in nature, in stones, in flowers, in people.

These thoughts were greatly encouraged by American activity, by the Phillips Memorial Gallery and by Dumbarton Oaks; homes made public and vital by continued enterprise. But how could this be managed without money? I tried for a 'Stately Home' which might become a source of interest to some neighbouring university and in the end was recommended by the President of the Cambridge Preservation Society, the use of four tiny condemned slum dwellings. So Kettle's Yard began. This was in 1957.

By keeping 'open house' every afternoon of term something was gradually developed which in 1966 was accepted by the University whose intention it was to continue this activity in its present form. On 5 May 1970 a large extension, designed by Sir Leslie Martin and his associates, was opened by His Royal Highness The Prince of Wales, and an inaugural concert was given by Jacqueline du Pré and Daniel Barenboim.

Kettle's Yard is in no way meant to be an art gallery or museum, nor is it simply a collection of works of art reflecting my taste or the taste of a given period. It is, rather, a continuing way of life from these last fifty years, in which stray objects, stones, glass, pictures, sculpture, in light and in space, have been used to make manifest the underlying stability which more and more we need to recognise if we are not to be swamped by all that is so rapidly opening up before us.

Jim Ede at his bureau in the downstairs sitting and dining room, undated photograph

There has always been this need, and I think there always will be; it is a condition of human life, and in Kettle's Yard, which should I think, grow and change only very slowly, I hope that future generations will still find a home and a welcome, a refuge of peace and order, of the visual arts and of music.

On my side, I have felt strongly my need to give to others these things which have so much been given to me; and to give in such a way that by their placing and by a pervading atmosphere one thing will enhance another, making perhaps a coherent whole, in which a continuity of enjoyment, in the constantly changing public of a university, can thrive. Perhaps from it other ventures of this sort may spring. There should be a Kettle's Yard in every university.

Reprinted from the *Handlist* of 1970

Introduction to Kettle's Yard

The junction of Northampton Street and Honey Hill, 1920s
looking across what is now the green towards Kettle's Yard

Jim Ede described Kettle's Yard as "a space, an ambience, a home". Jim and Helen Ede believed that art could be part of daily life. They wanted their collection of art and objects to be enjoyed in the relaxed domestic setting of their home and they felt that Kettle's Yard was "only alive when used". This introduction explores the history of the original site, Jim Ede's life, the development of Kettle's Yard from 1957 to 1973, and its subsequent transformation into one of the leading spaces to experience modern and contemporary art.

History of the Area

The area known as Kettle's Yard derived its name from the Kettle family. During the eighteenth century, the family built a popular theatre on the site, but this was promptly closed by the university authorities, on the grounds that it would corrupt the morals of the students. 'Kettle's Yard' gradually declined into one of the city's poorest areas, a place for small businesses and jobbing tradesmen. By the early twentieth century it was an overcrowded site made up of cottages, workshops, pubs and shops, and increasingly regarded as a slum.

After the Second World War, and in parallel with the postwar drive in Britain for urban reconstruction, the area underwent radical change. When new housing for elderly residents was built on Honey Hill, only four severely dilapidated cottages were spared through the efforts of the Cambridge Preservation Society. It was in this derelict state that Jim and Helen Ede first discovered the site in 1956.

Jim Ede: A Friend of Artists

The son of a solicitor from Cardiff, H. S. 'Jim' Ede (1895–1990) was sensitive to art and ideas of beauty from a young age. He spent a year with family in France in 1908, visiting Paris museums and discovering what he described as an elegance of living. This was followed by visiting the art collections of the Fitzwilliam Museum while a border at the Leys School in Cambridge between 1909 and 1912. After periods at art school in Cornwall and Edinburgh, Ede enlisted when war broke out, joining the South Wales Borderers. In 1916 he was sent back from the front suffering from physical and mental exhaustion. There is much to suggest that his experience of the trenches shaped Ede's life and his need

Jim Ede (left) with artist Italo Valenti in Switzerland, photograph c.1970s

to make spaces for art and people – sanctuaries – expressed most completely through Kettle's Yard.

Following time spent training officer cadets at Trinity College, Cambridge, Ede studied at the Slade School of Fine Art in London for a year and hoped to become a painter. In these years he developed a keen interest in Early Renaissance art. In 1921, Ede married Helen Schlapp, the daughter of a Professor of German at Edinburgh University, who he met when Helen was a student at Edinburgh School of Art. In the same year, needing to earn a living, but still wishing to work in close contact with art, he worked as a photographic assistant at the National Gallery. In 1922 Ede joined the National Gallery of British Art (renamed the Tate Gallery in 1932) as a curator and assistant to the Director specialising in working with contemporary art and artists.

During the 1920s, partly as a consequence of his work at Tate, Ede became close friends with artists including Ben and Winifred Nicholson, Christopher Wood and David Jones. Trips on official gallery business to Paris led to meetings with some of the key figures of the artistic avant-garde, including Pablo Picasso, Marc Chagall, Joan Miró and Constantin Brancusi. Ede often visited to these artists' studios. These encounters brought a contemporary awareness to Ede's interest in art and his friend-ships with artists played a central role in shaping his taste and approach to life. He later underlined this, by remarking that, above all, he would describe himself as 'a friend of artists'.

Central to Ede's burgeoning reputation as a connoisseur and collector was his acquisition, in 1927, of almost the entire estate contents of the French-born, but largely London-based, sculptor Henri Gaudier-Brzeska. Gaudier-Brzeska had been killed in action serving for the French army at the age of twenty-three in 1915. Ede strongly believed in the quality of the artist's work and was committed to promoting it: in 1930 he published a biography on Gaudier-Brzeska which was republished in 1931 as *Savage Messiah* and became a best-seller in Britain and the United States. The book remains a fundamental text for anyone interested in studying the artist. Ede contributed to the establishment of Gaudier-Brzeska's international reputation by supporting exhibitions and donating works to public collections in Britain and France.

All of these activities, combined with his secretaryship of the Contemporary Arts Society, resulted in an unremitting work-load, which exacerbated Ede's ongoing poor health. His unofficial role as the first modern art curator at the Tate was also at odds with the more conservative taste of the gallery's leadership. Accordingly, he resigned from both posts in 1936, beginning a very early professional 'retirement' at the age of forty-one. Over the next twenty years he lived with Helen in Tangier, Morocco, and the Loire Valley, in France, concentrating on lecturing and writing about art. Ede collected little art work during these years, but he continued to review books and exhibitions. He also opened up his home in Tangier, named 'Whitestone', as a weekend refuge for servicemen based in Gibraltar. In 1941, Ede began the first of three lecture tours in America. He lectured on a wide range of topics but focused on British artists. While in New York, in particular, he sought out other significant artists whose work would later form part of his collection including William Congdon and Richard Pousette-Dart. By the mid-1950s, a desire to be nearer to their children, Elisabeth and Mary, encouraged Jim and Helen to return to England. It was at this time that the need for a permanent home for the collection became foremost in Ede's mind.

Kettle's Yard 1957–73

In a 1956 letter to artist David Jones, Jim Ede wrote that:

> "It would be interesting to be lent a great house on the verge of a city – or a place of beauty in a town (Cambridge I have in mind) and make it all that I could of lived in beauty, each room an atmosphere of quiet and simple charm, and open to the public (in Cambridge to students especially) and for such a living creation I would give all that I have in pictures and lovely objects, would bear the initial cost of making the house suitable, give my services for the next 10 years … Helen and I would live in a bit of it. The rest would look lived in, and its special feature would be I think one of simplicity and loved qualities. There could be a library there (art perhaps) and there could be evenings of chamber music."

In Ede's vision, this house was to be:

> *"a living place where works of art would be enjoyed, inherent to the domestic setting, where young people could be at home unhampered by the greater austerity of the museum or public art gallery, and where an informality might infuse an underlying formality."*

Jim and Helen Ede's search for a suitable home commenced. They could not find an existing 'great house' in Cambridge and instead settled upon a project to transform the four derelict cottages of 'Kettle's Yard' in 1956. With the help of local architect Rowland De Winton Aldridge, the Edes restored and remodelled the existing early nineteenth century cottages and, in 1957, moved in.

The house was ready to receive visitors by the end of the year. Ede installed the collection of art, furniture, glass, ceramics and other objects that he had gathered throughout his lifetime. By carefully considering the precise position of each work of art and object, and their relationship with each other, he aimed to create a perfectly balanced whole, which would become almost a work of art in its own right. The notion of balance was central to Ede's vision, and encompassed his radical approach to found objects. Ede created a democracy of display, where everything is attributed equal visual importance. In 1984, he noted that "pebbles are as important as anything else".

Ede did not have a vast fortune at his disposal with which to purchase art. Instead, he often acquired works by exchange or through the generosity of his artist friends. He also purchased works by artists who were at the early stages of their careers and had not necessarily established themselves in the art market. The Ede's collection was one of outstanding quality and importance. As well as the Gaudier-Brzeska estate, which formed the backbone of the collection, it contained the most substantial publicly accessible holdings of early works by Ben and Winifred Nicholson and paintings by Christopher Wood. Moreover, the display of the Ede's collection of Alfred Wallis paintings helped to establish the painter's place in the history of art, as until then only a few individuals had recognised the quality of Wallis' work.

The practice of opening their home and engaging with new visitors, whatever their background, had its roots in the 1920s and 1930s, when Jim and Helen's home in Hampstead had attracted artists such as Georges Braque, Sergei Diaghilev, Vaslav Nijinsky, Naum Gabo, John Gielgud, Henry Moore, and Ben and Winifred Nicholson. The core of any day at Kettle's Yard, however, became the holding of 'open house' to university undergraduates on weekday afternoons. These were initially the people that Jim Ede really hoped to engage with the arts. This was partly the consequence of the democratising experience of lecturing to a variety of audiences during the Second World War. From this, Ede had developed the notion that each visitor could bring new life to the collection, thus also enhancing his own appreciation of it. In addition to students, the newly opened house soon began to attract artists working locally, such as Cecil Collins and Elisabeth Vellacott, who remembered that:

> *"When Jim first arrived in Cambridge few people, except for the small group of artists living here, were aware that they lacked any place where they could see and enjoy contemporary twentieth century art. The Fitzwilliam were not concerned. Jim was a beam of light to us."*

Partly as a consequence of Helen's poor health, the daily routine and organisation of the house fell largely to Jim. This pleased him, because it gave him direct control over the realisation of his vision of art in a domestic setting. In fact, the tasks of cleaning the house and re-positioning objects became a form of ritual with almost transcendental implications. He recalled that:

> *"Even the so-called chores I turn to joy; the sweeping of a floor, dust slanting in rays of light, the quality of wood or stone, the cleaning of a window, that thrilling, insubstantial substance glass, hard against driven rain, yet liquid to light."*

Ede's sense of the sacred in daily routines complements his vision of art as a means to spiritual growth. Since the early-1920s he had been deeply interested in the spiritual and had developed a particular fascination for Asian and Middle Eastern cultures. Such interest was enhanced by his friendship with the painter and poet David Jones, as well as during the 1950s, the American painters William Congdon and Richard Pousette-Dart. Each artist's work revolved, although in different ways, around transcendental concerns.

Handwritten notice inviting students to Kettle's Yard, c. 1968–70

KETTLE'S YARD
(OFF NORTHAMPTON ST)

PAINTINGS, SCULPTURE and DRAWINGS

Undergraduates are welcome to call any day, including Sundays, between 2 PM and 4 PM

Jim Ede.

The official handover date of Kettle's Yard from the Edes to the University of Cambridge was 30 November 1966. The university assumed responsibility for the building and the collection, but Jim and Helen continued to be resident and Jim retained the title of 'honorary curator'. Initially the gift of the collection to the university made little difference to the daily routine. But it soon became apparent that the house needed an extension to provide additional space for the growing collection, to meet Jim Ede's wish that music should have an important role in Kettle's Yard's life, and to accommodate temporary art exhibitions. A voluminous correspondent, Ede spent much of the later 1960s writing letters to individuals whom he thought might help to fund the project.

The house extension, designed by architects Leslie Martin and David Owers, was opened on 5 May 1970 with a concert by the world-renowned musicians Jacqueline du Pré and Daniel Barenboim. A piece of architecture that is imbued with light and space, the extension to the cottages represents a very successful materialisation of Ede's interest in natural light and its ever-changing interplay with objects and spaces. Created to counterbalance the more intimate conditions of the cottages, though sharing their domestic atmosphere, the extension also shows how modernist architecture can be successfully and gently joined to a historic building with reciprocal aesthetic and functional benefit.

When the extension opened, two things became clear: the diversity of Ede's collection, and its scale, something known only to close friends before this time. Ede had resumed collecting actively in the late 1950s, after a gap of some twenty years, and was concentrating on the work of younger artists such as Roger Hilton, William Scott and Italo Valenti, whose collages he acquired from Documenta III in 1964.

The new extension, however, added to the daily tasks required to keep Kettle's Yard in a presentable state and Ede began to call on student and volunteer help, as he was now in his mid seventies. Moreover, Helen's worsening health made it difficult for her to bear the daily pressure of visitors. In 1973, the Edes left Kettle's Yard entirely in the hands of the University and moved to Edinburgh, Helen's home city, where she died four years later. Jim spent his last years as a hospital visitor before his death in March 1990.

Jim Ede kept in very close touch with Kettle's Yard following his departure from Cambridge in 1973. He expected the same level of commitment from the new curators as he had shown. In a letter to an applicant for the job, he described the post as that of 'resident' and stressed the importance of committing oneself to 'make it live' for others.

Contemporary view of the cottages
from Northampton Street

Kettle's Yard Today
Jennifer Powell

Kettle's Yard still closely reflects Jim Ede's original vision. The story of the Kettle's Yard site after the Ede's departure is one of gradual transformation into the renowned house and gallery that it is today.

During his residency and between his departure and the publication of his book *A Way of Life* in 1984, Ede made some small changes to the display of the collection in the house. Indeed, writing to the curator Jeremy Lewison in 1980, he notes that the positions of objects 'may be altered from time to time'. Its arrangement, however, is maintained as far as possible as we believe Ede intended, as was his expressed desire when he gifted the collection to the university. The house is still open every day except on Mondays and the high-quality music programme established by Ede has continued to develop to include chamber concerts, contemporary music and student recitals. The loan collection, through which Ede enabled students to borrow pictures to hang in their own rooms, extended the principle of art as part of everyday experience throughout the University and continues to be available to students. With generous support from the Friends of Kettle's Yard and other funding bodies, the house and collection are conserved and preserved for the enjoyment of current and future generations.

The adjoining gallery that was built as part of the 1970 extension, was enlarged twice in the 1980s and a third time in 1993–94. This process enabled the expansion of a high quality modern and contemporary art exhibition programme and educational initiatives at Kettle's Yard. Despite an ambitious programme, these spaces were still relatively small, particularly for visiting school groups. In 2004 Jamie Fobert Architects were commissioned to begin work on a new Education Wing under the Directorship of Michael Harrison. This project was extended to encompass the gallery and public spaces, which were also in much need of renovation, by the current Director Andrew Nairne in 2012.

Looking Ahead

The new spaces that Jamie Fobert and his team designed opened on 10 February 2018. Their light and volume, together with carefully chosen materials, create close conversations between the old and new spaces.

Jamie Fobert's architecture has helped to bring Kettle's Yard's site together as one. The connectivity between the house, its ethos and the new spaces, underpins the approach to the programme in 2018 and beyond. Kettle's Yard continues to stage research-led exhibitions that take their starting point from the collection. Ede's ethos of openness and access is at the very heart of what we do. Kettle's Yard aims to be a place that welcomes those who have never been to a gallery before, as well as frequent visitors. The new 2018 Education Wing allowed us to extend further our programme of talks, events, and art making activities to reach wider and more diverse audiences and to interact in innovative ways with the world-leading university of which we are a central part.

At the core of Kettle's Yard's exhibition, event and learning programme is supporting the best of contemporary art and artists in the UK and internationally. This approach is directly inspired by Ede's passion for living artists. Kettle's Yard stages ambitious contemporary art exhibitions today that reflect and support the art of our time, as well as some contemporary interventions in the house and in the adjacent St Peter's Church.

At Kettle's Yard we believe that art is for everyone and our activity is informed by Ede's belief in the power of art to make us look again. Our aim is for the house and collection, the exhibitions in our galleries and our extensive archive to be resources which inspire artists, curators, students, researchers and all of our visitors. We hope that you enjoy exploring this unique house and gallery, and that you might want to return again and bring your friends and family with you. As Jim Ede suggested in a letter of 1964:

> *"Do come in as often as you like – the place is only alive when used"*.

Cottages: Sitting and Dining Room

Alfred Wallis
1 *Four-masted schooner and lighthouse*, undated
Oil on wood

David Jones
2 *The Four Queens (reproduction)*, 1941
Off-set print on paper

Unknown
3 Pre-Columbian head, undated
Stone

David Jones
4 *Seascape from a Terrace*, 1929
Watercolour on paper

Ben Nicholson
5 *jug*, 1967
Etching on paper

David Peace
6 *Glass goblet 'Achoellen Bremblens'*, 1971
Engraved glass

John Acland
7 *Carving*, c. 1960
Slate

Ian Hamilton Finlay
8 KETTLE'S YARD /
CAMBRIDGE /
ENGLAND IS THE /
LOUVRE OF
THE PEBBLE, 1995
Inscribed stone

Unknown
9 Chief's seat, from Atiu,
Cook Islands, undated
Wood

Christopher Wood
10 *Flowers*, 1930
Oil on board

11 *Paris Snow Scene*, 1926
Oil on canvas

12 *Ship in Harbour*, 1928
Incised wash on board

Elisabeth Vellacott
13 *Trees, Orchard in Spring*, 1967
Graphite on paper

William Congdon
14 *Istanbul no.2*, 1953
Oil on board

Ben Nicholson
15 *1927 (apples and pears)*, 1927
Oil and graphite on canvas

Alfred Wallis
16 *Seascape – ships sailing past the Longships*, c. 1928
Oil on canvas

Christopher Wood
17 *Le Phare*, 1930
Oil on board

Joan Miró
18 *Tic Tic*, 1927
Oil on canvas

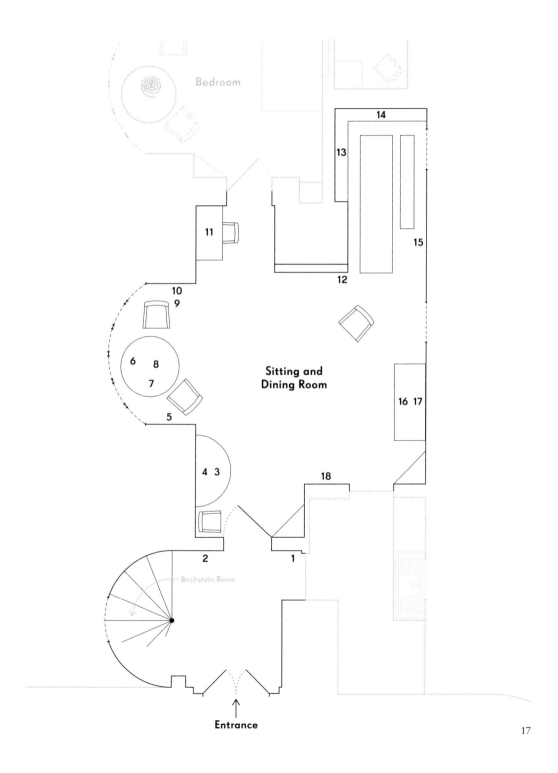

Bedroom

14

13

11

15

12

Sitting and
Dining Room

10
9

6   8
7

16 17

5

4 3

18

2

1

Bechstein Room

Entrance

17

View of the sitting room

Jim Ede's sitting room introduces some of the recurring visual themes of Kettle's Yard. Relationships between art and found objects, light and dark, smooth and textured surfaces are central to this space. Light floods in through the slatted blinds, creating patterns on the floor that gradually fade into the shadow of the recessed dining area. Ede was especially interested in exploiting the variations in angle and intensity of the sunlight to create changing visual effects. When Ede was refurbishing the cottages he added bay windows in this and the next room, to allow more light.

On the round table by the window, the intersecting circles of John Acland's **Carving [7]** echo the relationship between the semicircles of the windows and the table by the entrance door. The subtle use of light is also a significant feature in David Jones' **Seascape from a Terrace [4]**, an early watercolour by the poet-artist. The view is painted from the house that his parents regularly rented at Portslade, on the coast near Brighton. The artist recalled: "… the bungalows were remarkable in that they were built literally on the sea-margin, so that if the weather were at all rough, the surf and spray broke on their seaward balconies – and I made numerous drawings looking wave-ward." The series focused on the motif of the sea seen from an interior, a subject which the artist investigated again in Wales and Devon. The bureau standing at the opening to Ede's bedroom was his first purchase at the age of fourteen. It was where he conducted all of his business during his period of residency at Kettle's Yard between 1957 and 1973.

Ben Nicholson's **1927 (apples and pears) [15]** hangs at the entrance to the dining area. Like the majority of the artist's paintings at Kettle's Yard, it dates from the early part of his career. Ede could afford to buy Nicholson's paintings only until the 1930s; in the following decades the artist's success made them too expensive for him. This is why the majority of later works by Nicholson in the collection are either drawings or prints, many of them gifts from the artist. An indication of the care Ede took in the disposition of paintings can be found in the progression from light to dark between Nicholson's luminous *1927 (apples and pears)*, displayed in full light, and William Congdon's **Istanbul no.2 [14]**, hanging at the dark end of the dining area.

Sitting room table with John Acland's *Carving* and David Peace's *Glass goblet 'Acho ellen Brembles'*

Another deliberate juxtaposition, although with a different intent, is the positioning of Christopher Wood's **Le Phare [17]** above Alfred Wallis' **Seascape (ships sailing past the Longships) [16]**. Liverpool-born Wood (1901–30) spent part of his short life in Paris, where he was introduced to the innovations of the avant-garde. In 1928, while in St Ives with Ben Nicholson, he encountered the art of Alfred Wallis, a fisherman and scrap-metal merchant who had turned to painting in his seventies after his wife's death. Wallis' work had a strong impact on Wood: he bought at least sixteen paintings from him including *Seascape*, and wrote of "more and more influence de Wallis – not a bad master though." *Le Phare* combines a representation of the rough sea and the simply rendered fishing boat with the sophistication of Parisian-inspired still life painting, represented by the playing cards and the Breton newspaper in the foreground. Across the room and above Ede's bureau, Wood's **Paris Snow Scene [11]** suggests an interest in the work of Raoul Dufy, as well as enthusiasm for the dynamics of urban life.

Ede found his concerns with balance echoed in Joan Miró's painting **Tic Tic [18]**:

> "The Miró was to me an opportunity to show under-graduates the importance of balance. If I put my finger over the spot at the top right all the rest of the picture slid into the left-hand bottom corner. If I covered the one at the bottom, horizontal lines appeared, and if somehow I could take out the tiny red spot in the middle everything flew to the edges. This gave me a much needed chance to mention God, and by saying that if I had another name for God, I think it would be balance, for with perfect balance all would be well."

A wooden cider press screw supporting two glass decanters stands below the Miró. Ede loved the effects that glass and crystal could have on an interior. He described one arrangement of goblets and glasses in the upstairs extension as "being like a golden city".

The tight spiral of the cider screw prepares the eye for the spiral of the staircase to the first floor and is reminiscent of some of the wooden bases used by Constantin Brancusi for his sculptures. The atmosphere of Brancusi's studio, which Ede had visited in the 1920s, was one of the formative influences on Kettle's Yard. Ede wrote that when he went there he had felt that:

"... all the elements were there collected in his studio, almost as though it were nature's workshop. There I found air and light, and the poise and rhythm of his carvings ... I pulled a string outside the door and a hammer hit upon a disc of brass within, making a lovely echoing sound. When Brancusi opened the door it was still vibrating. 'People bring me music while they wait' he said."

Joan Miró, *Tic Tic*, 1927, above a cider press and two glass decanters

Cottages: Bedroom and Bathroom

Ben Nicholson

1   *1934 (relief)*, 1934
    Oil, graphite and coloured card

2   *sexagonal*, 1967
    Engraving on paper

Henri Gaudier-Brzeska

3   *Torpedo Fish (Toy)*, 1914
    (posthumous cast, 1968)
    Bronze

Ben Nicholson

4   *1952 (goblet)*, 1952
    Engraving, ink, graphite
    and wash on cardboard

5   *1928 (Cornish port)*, 1928
    Oil on card

6   *1945 (boats in
    St Ives Harbour)*, 1945
    Graphite on paper

William Congdon

7   *Moonlight Subiaco*, 1967
    Graphite on paper

Jane Adams

8   *Two girls, one with a doll*, 1955
    Graphite and crayon on paper

Henri Gaudier-Brzeska

9   *Door-Knocker*, 1914
    Carved brass

William Congdon

10   *Piazza San Marco no. 5*
     Oil on hardboard

Ben Nicholson

11   *letters and numbers*, c. 1933
     Linocut on cloth

Christopher Wood

12   *Landscape at Vence*, 1927
     Oil on canvas

Alfred Wallis

13   *Grey steam boat*, undated
     Oil and graphite on card

14   *Three masted barque with
     three small ships*, undated
     Oil on card

William Congdon

15   *Guatemala no. 7
     (Dying Vulture)*, 1957
     Oil on hardboard

Alfred Wallis

16   *Houses at the water's edge
     (Porthleven)*, c. 1925–28
     Oil and graphite on card

17   *Five ships
     (Mount's Bay)*, c. 1928
     Oil and graphite on card

Henry Moore

18   *Head*, 1928
     Stone on plaster base

Ben Nicholson

19   *1941 (abstract)*, 1941
     Gouache on board

David Jones

20   *Vexilla Regis*, 1948
     Graphite and watercolour
     on paper

Henri Gaudier-Brzeska

21   *Duck*, 1914
     Serpentine stone

22   *Duck*, 1914
     Bronze

23   *Head*, 1912
     Marble
     On loan to Kettle's Yard

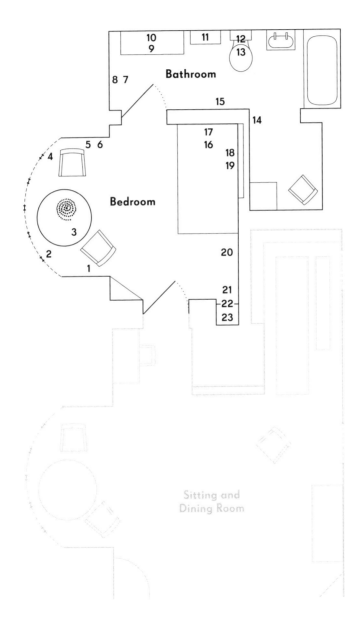

Bathroom

Bedroom

Sitting and
Dining Room

Table showing spiral
of stones and
Henri Gaudier-Brzeska's
Torpedo Fish (Toy)

The tabletop arrangement sets the tone for the whole of Jim Ede's bedroom. The spiral of stones and the spherical green glass float complement the linear patterns of the table and echo its circular shape. These, and the shells, underline the importance of found and natural objects at Kettle's Yard as a complement to works of art. The resemblance of the stone spiral to a mandala, the Buddhist and Hindu instrument of meditation representing the Universe, is also significant, given Ede's lifelong interest in spirituality.

Next to the spiral stands the first of many works by Henri Gaudier-Brzeska to be seen in the house, the small, angular **Torpedo Fish (Toy) [3]**. This work was originally made for the philosohper T. E. Hulme. The sculpture fuses concerns of a machine aesthetic with the representation of nature. A similar combination is apparent in **Duck [22]**, a carving made in serpentine stone, situated in the corner cupboard, and the carved brass **Door-Knocker [9]**, on the dresser in the bathroom.

Carved from Shakespeare's Cliff chalk, Henry Moore's early stone **Head [18]**, a gift from the sculptor in 1957, is a rare surviving example of several such works from the 1920s. Like Gaudier-Brzeska, Moore looked at non-Western and pre-Renaissance forms to break with an exhausted sculptural tradition, and he studied the ethnographic collections of the British Museum and the sculpture collections at the Victoria and

Albert Museum. The acquisition of this sculpture just before work began on Kettle's Yard allowed Ede to create a special place for it in his bedroom, the most personal room in the house, alongside works by Gaudier-Brzeska, David Jones, Ben Nicholson and Alfred Wallis.

The positioning of Ben Nicholson's **1928 (Cornish port) [5]** almost at floor level – a feature often found in the house – shows how Ede regarded rooms as spaces to be enjoyed at different heights, while sitting down as well as standing. The work dates from the summer of the artist's celebrated first encounter with Alfred Wallis in St Ives. The simple representation of the sailing boat, the use of deep blue and red and the use of a scrap of board all seem to mark a response to Wallis' work, although Nicholson had already shown an interest in a simplified approach to form.

Ede repeatedly acknowledged the importance of Ben Nicholson in the shaping of his taste in the 1920s. One of the artist's stylistic traits that particularly appealed to Ede was his restrained palette, a quality shared with Wallis. Writing on Wallis, Nicholson once stated that "he used very few colours, and one associates

View showing Jim Ede's bed with works by Alfred Wallis, Henry Moore and Ben Nicholson

with him some lovely dark browns, shiny blacks, fierce greys, strange whites and a particularly pungent Cornish green." Nicholson developed an almost instant admiration for Wallis, and promptly introduced Ede to his work. Ede responded very enthusiastically and in 1928 he wrote that "you can't expect me to pay much attention to pictures by Ben Nicholson or by Winifred Nicholson when you send me this by Wallis."

The presence of Wallis' paintings above Ede's bed emphasises the importance that he attached to them. **Five ships (Mount's Bay) [16]** and **Houses at the water's edge (Porthleven) [17]**, employ maritime subjects and are executed in unevenly applied boat paint, with blunt outlines and distortion of scale that typifies Wallis' style. Wallis painted from memory and both Ede and Nicholson were fascinated by the freshness of experience and perception that he demonstrated in his works.

David Jones' drawing, **Vexilla Regis [20]**, positioned on the wall next to the glass cupboard, is a dense network of pencilled lines and muted colour. The intense detail is typical of Jones' style in the late 1940s, and the layers of spiritual and historical meaning are also characteristic. In a 1949 letter to Ede's mother, who had bought the drawing, the artist recalled its origins:

> "... the main jumping off ground was, I think, a Latin hymn we sing as part of the Good Friday Liturgy in the Roman rite ... starting Vexilla Regis prodeunt 'Forth come the standards of the King,' a very ancient processional hymn, in which are many allusions to the tree and the Cross and to the Cross as a tree ... The general idea of the picture was also associated, in my mind, with the collapse of the Roman World."

The drawing alludes to Jones' service with the Royal Welsh Fusiliers in the Great War, and in particular to the assault on Mametz Wood, where he was injured in July 1916. The horses make reference to an episode in Sir Thomas Malory's *Morte d'Arthur* when, after the death of Guenevere and the break-up of the Round Table, Lancelot and other knights let their horses free to roam – an example of the artist's fascination with Arthurian legend and Celtic Britain. Jones' deep engagement with religious matters was of great interest to Ede. Significantly, the artist shared with Jim the sense of the elevation of routine daily tasks, such as cleaning, to an almost sacred status.

Jim's bathroom displays a varied group of works, including Christopher Wood's Van Gogh-inspired **Landscape at Vence [12]**, Ben Nicholson's fabric print **letters and numbers [11]** and William Congdon's **Guatemala no.7 (Dying Vulture) [15]**. Ede's delight in art as an everyday experience, touching the lives of all, is evident in the positioning of a drawing by his granddaughter, Jane Adams, behind the bathroom door.

Bathroom dresser with Henri Gaudier-Brzeska's *Door-Knocker* and above this William Congdon's *Piazzo San Marco no. 5.* Adjacent is Ben Nicholson's *letters and numbers*

Cottages: Bechstein Room

Unknown
1   Venetian Mirror, 18th Century

Unknown
2   Yak bell and stand,
    Tibetan, 19th Century
    Wood, metal and leather

David Jones
3   *Flora in Calix-Light*, 1950
    Graphite and watercolour
    on paper

Unknown
4   Modern Aborigine flints

Italo Valenti
5   *Cervi volanti;*
    Cerfs-volant, 1964
    Paper collage and
    watercolour on paper

David Jones
6   *Lourdes*, 1928
    Watercolour on paper

Henri Gaudier-Brzeska
7   *Sleeping Fawn*, 1913
    (posthumous cast, 1960)
    Bronze

Lucie Rie
8   *Bowl*, 1950s
    Terracotta, glazed

Ben Nicholson
9   *1928 (Banks Head –*
    Cumbrian landscape), 1928
    Oil on canvas

10 *1932–33 (black guitar)*,
    1932–33
    Oil on canvas

Alfred Wallis
11 *Schooner on a blue sea*, undated
    Oil and graphite on card

Francine Del Pierre
12 *Bowl*, 1960s
    Terracotta, glazed

Richard Pousette-Dart
13 *Group of brass rings and*
    one jade ring, c. 1940–50
    Brass and jade
    (now often displayed
    in Helen's Bedroom)

Alfred Wallis
14 *Three sailing boats*
    in a line, undated
    Oil on paper mounted on card

Roger Hilton
15 *October 1955 Calm*
    (Black, Grey, Brown
    and White), 1955
    Oil on canvas

Constantin Brancusi
16 *Nude*, c. 1920–25
    Pen and ink on paper

17 *Prometheus*, 1912
    Cement cast

Laurence Whistler
18 *Untitled*, 1974
    Window engraving

Ben Nicholson
19 *1948 (three pears)*, 1948
    Graphite on paper

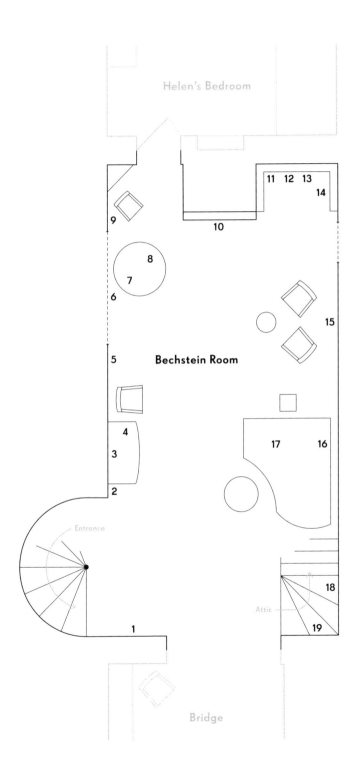

Helen's Bedroom

11 12 13

14

9

10

8

7

6

15

5 **Bechstein Room**

4

3

17 16

2

Entrance

18

Attic

19

1

Bridge

This area used to be Helen Ede's main sitting room. It introduces a theme that is fundamental to Kettle's Yard – music and its relationship with the visual arts. This is emphasised by the display of Ben Nicholson's **1932–33 (black guitar) [10]** and Brancusi's **Prometheus [17]** on top of the Bechstein piano, a juxtaposition that is echoed in the ground floor of the extension by the positioning of Nicholson's *1933 (musical instruments)* and Naum Gabo's *Linear Construction in Space No. 1* which usually sits on the Steinway piano.

Prometheus, in Greek mythology one of the Titans and god of fire, tricked Zeus, the chief god, into accepting the bones and fat of sacrifice instead of the meat. When Zeus hid fire from man to punish him, Prometheus stole it and returned it to Earth once again. As punishment, Zeus had him chained to a rock and sent an eagle to eat his liver, which constantly replenished itself. In Brancusi's 1912 interpretation of Prometheus' tragic fate, this head – a portrait of an actual child – is inclined in a gesture that suggests both pain and eternal rest. The sculptor often attempted to balance the themes of sleep and torment in his art. Here the title might refer to the idea of Prometheus as the original artist, a creator defiant of the gods, which had been taken up by the German Romantics and was familiar to Brancusi. This cement cast, after a marble original made in 1911, is one of several versions in different materials of the work. The features of the head barely emerge from the cement. The smooth surface is offset by the reflections on the piano. This gives the viewer a real sense

View of the
Bechstein room

Dresser with David Jones'
Flora in Calix-Light

of the volume of the object, though at the same time making
it appear floating, thus creating a tension between weight and
lightness. The interplay of the work with light and reflective
surfaces is part of the visual construction that characterises this
room. Once again here Ede carefully arranged light and dark,
in a sequence that leads the eye from the window by the staircase
to the Venetian mirror, to David Jones' luminous **Flora in Calix-
Light [3]**, followed by Prometheus' delicate reflections through
to Ben Nicholson's *1932–33 (black guitar)* and the dark opening
of the fireplace.

　　The other dominant feature in this room is the juxtaposition
of works with a markedly spiritual content, although with a variety
of connotations. A direct association of art and religion emerges
from David Jones' watercolour *Flora in Calix-Light*, on the wall
opposite the piano. Born in South London in 1895, Jones had been
associated with Eric Gill's communities of artists and craftsmen in
Sussex and Wales in the 1920s, working as an engraver and printer,
while at the same time writing poetry and essays. His Catholic faith
played an important role in his artistic development. Ede shared
Jones' interest in religion and the friendship between the two
lasted until the artist's death. In *Flora in Calix-Light* ('calix' is the
Latin word for 'chalice') the three glass goblets of flowers, placed
on a highly polished table, slowly emerge from the surface of
the work and may refer to the Holy Trinity. In addition to Catholic

31

symbolism, the curving serpentine outline of the flowers and window latches seem to allude to Celtic decoration, thus reflecting Jones' interest in his own Welsh origins.

The two Ben Nicholson paintings provide an insight into the development of his art between the late 1920s and early 1930s. **1928 (Banks Head – Cumbrian landscape) [9]** was painted at Banks Head, the farmhouse near Carlisle that he shared with his first wife Winifred. The work demonstrates the Nicholson's attempt to capture a spontaneity that was often associated with the art of children or untrained artists and described as Naïve art. The speed of work in the sketchy details laid over the green ground in a very limited range of colours accords with Winifred's practice. Some critics familiar with his later abstract works were uneasy with such an apparent lack of formal organisation. However, Nicholson's tendency to compose around areas of detail and space can be seen in the pressing of the hedgerows to top and bottom.

1932–33 (black guitar), on the other hand, reflects Ben Nicholson's interest in the Cubist still life paintings of Georges Braque. The surface of the painting is very heavily scored, with linear incisions crossing over the form of the guitar itself. This creates a relief-like effect, enhanced by the lightening of the tones on the sides of the guitar, which brings the instrument forward to the front of the picture. The rhythms of the incised lines seem to suggest the rasping excitement of a flamenco guitar. The artist's interest in line, subtle spatial arrangement and cutting into the surface of his works was to lead to the pure abstraction of his white reliefs of the mid-1930s.

Nicholson's focus on still life and objects matched Ede's interest. On the mantelpiece, a dried out seed pod placed on a pebble and a grey-yellow patterned plate once thought to be by William 'Quaker' Pegg can be found. These, together with the Dutch engraved glass and other natural objects, are composed almost as elements in a still life painting. The brass and jade rings on top of the bookcase were made by the American painter and sculptor Richard Pousette-Dart, a friend and correspondent of Jim's, particularly during the 1940s and 1950s. Pousette-Dart was one of the artists associated with the emergence of Abstract Expressionism in New York. He was interested in the life and work of Gaudier-Brzeska, especially the artist's abstract brass and stone carvings.

Cottages: Helen's Bedroom and Bathroom

**Naum Gabo and
Ben Nicholson**

1   Wall-case containing sculptures by
Naum Gabo dating from the late
1930s to the early 1970s and paintings
by Ben Nicholson of the 1930s

Unknown

2   *Kurdistan embroidered trouser*
Textile

Alfred Wallis

3   *French lugsail fishing boat*, undated
Oil on card

Ben Nicholson

4   *Brissago*, 1965
Etching on paper

Zoë Ellison

5   *Bowl*, (filled with pebbles), c. 1950s
Earthenware

Alfred Wallis

6   *Small boat in a rough sea*, c. 1936
Oil on card

David Jones

7   *Tailpiece for
'The Ancient Mariner'*, 1928
Engraving on paper

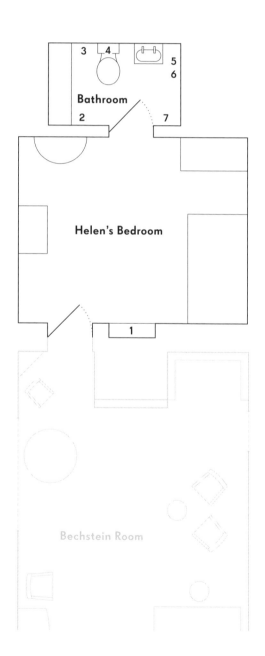

Helen Schlapp first met Jim Ede when she was a student at Edinburgh College of Art. They married in 1921. During the Ede's residence at Kettle's Yard, Helen's bedroom and bathroom were usually closed to the visiting public. They remained Helen's private space. The bedroom was used as an office after the Ede's departure, and it was not integrated with the rest of the house until the late 1980s. Whilst the arrangement of mugs, pebbles and works by Alfred Wallis and David Jones in the bathroom rarely alters, the bedroom space is used frequently today for changing displays and contemporary projects.

Helen Ede's bedroom during the display *Grace and Speed* in 2015

These displays include loaned works by artists whom Ede admired or were contemporaneous with others in the collection and, more frequently, displays of works from the Kettle's Yard reserve collection. In 2015 our young people's group Circuit (aged 15–25) curated a display of drawings in this space by Henri Gaudier-Brzeska entitled *Grace and Speed* which coincided with the exhibition *New Rhythms: Henri Gaudier-Brzeska* in the main galleries.

The bedroom is also used as a space to support contemporary artists who are invited to show work and make interventions within it. Examples of such projects include a display of

Vicken Parsons' (born 1957) recent paintings in 2014. As was the case with Parsons' project, small numbers of works can sometimes also be found in other rooms in the house. As part of the re-opening exhibition in 2018, *Actions. The image of the world can be different*, the artist Cornelia Parker (born 1956) created a new drawing in chalk directly on the windows of the bedroom.

There is a small wall-case in the bedroom adjacent to the bed which usually houses a display of sculptures by Naum Gabo ranging in date from the late 1930s to the early 1970s, many of which were given to Kettle's Yard by his family in 2007, and a number of exquisite small painted works by Ben Nicholson.

Direct carving and the use of stone did not fit obviously within the constructive principles that Naum Gabo had developed early in his career when he favoured working in metals. His interest in carving started in the 1930s, and intensified after his move to London in 1936 and during the Second World War when he was living in St Ives. In England he met Barbara Hepworth and Henry Moore who were also employing this technique. From the mid 1930s, Gabo experimented with the use of Perspex and stringing in his sculptures to explore space, light and volume. In the following decades, and especially in the 1960s when Gabo was living in America, he continued to make carved works along-side the larger scale constructions for which he is best known. These smaller carvings often resulted from his practice of reworking pebbles and stones, some of which he had collected in England.

Helen Ede's bedroom
containing a display
of works from the
reserve collection
including William Scott's
painting, *Still Life
with White Mug*, 1957

Cottages: Attic

You can find a list of works in the space or please ask one of our Visitor Assistants.

Sculptures

Henri Gaudier-Brzeska

1   *Samson and Delilah (Embracers)*, 1913
    Plaster cast

Ovidiu Maitec

2   *Bird*, c. 1969
    Walnut wood

Henri Gaudier-Brzeska

3   *Portrait of Major Smythies*, 1912
    (posthumous cast, 1971)
    Bronze

4   *Seated Woman*, 1914
    (posthumous cast, 1964)
    Bronze

Unknown

5   Skull from Henri Gaudier-Brzeska's
    studio, undated
    Stone

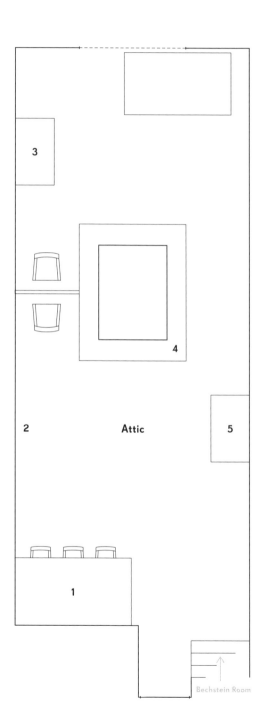

View of the attic showing Henri Gaudier-Brzeska's sculpture, *Seated Woman*, and above this his sketches, *Ezra Pound* and *Two men wrestling*

The attic displays a wide selection of works on paper and some sculptures by the French-born artist Henri Gaudier-Brzeska (1891–1915). By the age of twenty-three, Gaudier-Brzeska had made approximately 2000 works on paper and 115 sculptures. He was a self-taught artist who moved to London from Paris in 1911, but was tragically killed serving in the French army in 1915. A later bronze cast of one of the artist's last sculptures that was originally carved in marble in 1914, is displayed in the attic – **Seated Woman [4]** (another cast of this work is displayed in the downstairs extension).

Kettle's Yard has the largest collection of works by Gaudier-Brzeska, after Jim Ede acquired the vast majority of the artist's estate. This followed the passing of Gaudier-Brzeska's partner, Sophie Brzeska who had no heirs. Ede was working at the Tate Gallery at this time and organised the acquisition of a small number of works by national collections including Tate's own. However, the majority were declined and Ede purchased the remaining works in 1927.

The drawings in the attic are frequently rotated in order to preserve their condition and low lighting is also adopted for this purpose. A printed list of the works on paper that are currently on

Henri Gaudier-Brzeska,
*Self-Portrait with
a Pipe (3)*, 1913

display will be available on the table as you enter the attic. The sculptures displayed in this space are detailed on the adjacent map.

Henri Gaudier-Brzeska was born in Saint-Jean-de-Braye, France in 1891. He first visited London in the summer of 1906 and visited other UK cities between 1907 and 1909 whilst on a work scholarship studying business. In 1910 he met Sophie Brzeska in Paris and in the same year decided to devote himself to pursuing a career as an artist. The young couple moved to London in January 1911. It was at this time that Henri Gaudier added Sophie's surname to his own. Gaudier-Brzeska frequently visited the British Museum and was influenced by African art and art of other world cultures including Chinese calligraphy. After working in isolation for some time, Gaudier-Brzeska built up a circle of friends which included the poet Ezra Pound whom he sketched, the philosopher T. E. Hulme and fellow artists Percy Wyndham Lewis and Horace Brodzky. In the following years he became involved with Roger Fry's Omega Workshops and Pound's and Lewis' pioneering Vorticist group, contributing to the two issues of their magazine BLAST. This group promoted new and increasingly abstract art forms that they felt reflected the age of rapid change in which they were working.

Gaudier-Brzeska most frequently drew figures and animals; his treatment of these, and other subjects, ranged from closely observed and detailed studies such as *Grace and Speed, or the Golden Eagle's Wing* (1908) (which is one of Gaudier-Brzeska's earliest surviving drawings), to witty caricatures, to sketches in which he experimented with abstracted forms. In London he most often sketched quickly and moved rapidly between different styles even whilst exploring the same subject. The series of three *Self Portraits with a Pipe* (1, 2, 3) (1913) show the transformation from a naturalistic to a Cubist-inspired portrayal, with an exercise in abstraction that reveals the artist's interest in developing a new formal approach. In the portraits Gaudier-Brzeska self-consciously announces himself as an avant-garde artist.

Gaudier-Brzeska was a prolific draughtsman. He sketched wherever he went and particularly yearned for subjects in action: boxers, swordfighters, even animals fighting; dancers, women striding through the park with skirts blown by a gust of wind, birds landing on water. In the life drawing studio which he attended, Gaudier-Brzeska wanted the models to move around – to walk, run and dance, and when they did not, he moved instead. In the wresting studio, which he visited in 1912, he watched as men turned in the air and attempted to capture the physicality of their bodies.

Gaudier-Brzeska was a notable proponent of direct carving in sculpture – a method of making that privileged the natural qualities of the material (usually stone in Gaudier-Brzeska's's case) and often without preliminary studies. However, Gaudier-Brzeska often made works on paper that were tied in closely to his sculptures. There are numerous drawings for his iconic Vorticist sculpture *Bird Swallowing a Fish* (p.58). One of these drawings is a preparatory sketch composed of a small number of simple pencil lines that capture the energy and movement that Gaudier-Brzeska often sought in his works; another (illustrated below), is a highly contrasting detailed pen and ink study probably made after the finished sculpture. It is composed of geometric shapes and rhythmical planes that characterize Gaudier-Brzeska's Vorticist works. Other interesting examples of studies that related to Gaudier-Brzeska's sculptures can be found in the series of sketches that relate to the *Wrestlers relief* on display by the piano in the extension.

In 1912 Gaudier-Brzeska stated that "movement is the translation of life, and if art depicts life, movement should come into art, since we are only aware of it because it moves". He constantly sought subjects that were alive and his works on paper and sculptures reflect his incessant search for new forms.

Henri Gaudier-Brzeska,
Sketch of Bird Swallowing a Fish, 1914

Cottages: Bridge and Dancer Room

Henri Gaudier-Brzeska
1   *Dog*, 1914
    (posthumous cast 1965)
    Bronze

Ben Nicholson
2   *1958 (jugs 'criss cross')*, 1958
    Graphite and watercolour
    on card

John Blackburn
3   *Lead relief*, c. 1963
    Lead and oil mounted on wood

Michael Pine
4   *Construction*, 1955
    Plaster

Elisabeth Vellacott
5   *Portrait of Gwen Raverat*, 1954
    Pencil on paper

Tam MacPhail
6   *Construction*, c. 1968
    Iron

William Congdon
7   *Naples – Church*, 1950
    Oil on hardboard

Ben Nicholson
8   *letter and numbers*, c. 1933
    Linocut on cloth

Lucie Rie
9   *Bowl (brown and
    white inlaid line)*, 1974
    Porcelain

Kenji Umeda
10 *Spirality*, c. 1970–75
    Marble

William Scott
11 *Bowl (White on Grey)*, 1962
    Oil on canvas

Ben Nicholson
12 *1928–9 (two mugs)*, 1928–29
    Linocut on paper

Max Ernst
13 *Figure*, 1925
    Graphite on paper

Christopher Wood
14 *Landscape with Figures*, c. 1926
    Oil on canvas

Henri Gaudier-Brzeska
15 *Dancer*, 1913
    (posthumous cast, 1967)
    Bronze

George Kennethson
16 *Construction (Birds)*, c. 1968
    Staffordshire Alabaster

William Congdon
17 *Luna 7, Subiaco*, 1967
    Oil on hardboard

18 *Piazza San Marco no.25*, 1957
    Oil on hardboard

Simon Kenrick
19 *Design (Stonehenge)*, undated
    Collage and oil on board

Henri Gaudier-Brzeska
20 *Mermaid*, 1912–13
    Marble

Henri Gaudier-Brzeska
21 *Head*, 1913
    (posthumous cast 1964)
    Stone cast

Ben Nicholson
22 *1944 (mugs)*, 1944
    Oil and graphite on board

William Staite Murray
23 *Jar (The Heron)*, c. 1928
    Stoneware, glazed

Gregorio Vardanega
24 *Disc*, c. 1960
    Plexiglass

25 *Spherical Construction*, c. 1963
    Plexiglass

Ian Hamilton Finlay
26 *The Land's Shadows*, 1987
    Glass

Elisabeth Vellacott
27 *Bare Trees and Hills*, c. 1966
    Graphite on paper

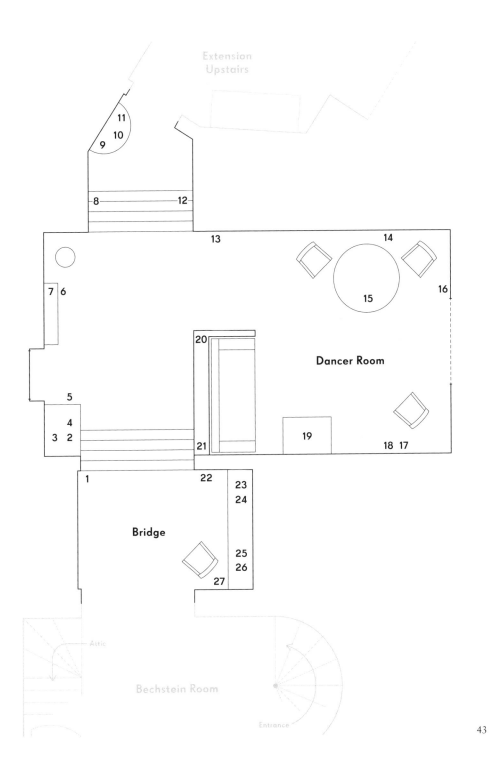

Extension
Upstairs

Dancer Room

Bridge

Attic

Bechstein Room

Entrance

43

The small conservatory of plants just before the stairs, highlights the importance placed by Jim Ede on the presence of nature amongst his collection. The interspersing of greenery, shells, stones and works of art reminds us that Ede viewed his collection as a living and ever-changing entity. The moving patterns of light and shadows across the surface of Gregorio Vardanega's plexiglass **Disc [24]**, suspended from the ceiling, further enhance this.

To the right of the conservatory hangs Elisabeth Vellacott's **Bare Trees and Hills [27]**, the first of her works acquired by Ede. Vellacott was born in 1905 and was a founder member of the Cambridge Society of Painters and Sculptors. What made this work particularly appealing to Ede was the fact that the artist "could leave untouched a large area of paper and yet keep it full. Never in the drawing itself does the paper become empty, so subtly does she approach it with her pencil." On the floor on the opposite side of the room stands Vellacott's **Portrait of Gwen Raverat [5]**, another Cambridge artist, best known for her wood engraving illustrations.

By the window stands **Jar (The Heron) [23]**, a tall vase by William Staite Murray. Ede remembered that:

> *"it had just been given to me by its maker ... when David Jones came to stay and knocked it off the window-sill of his bedroom. It was in several pieces. With much anxiety I told W.S.M., but he was delighted since it gave him the opportunity to mend it in the traditional way with gold."*

The adjacent space, known as the 'dancer room', is host to the most dramatic play of sunlight at Kettle's Yard. The large arched window, installed by Ede himself, casts changing patterns of raking light.

The two sculptures placed near the window are particularly affected by this light. George Kennethson's abstract **Construction (Birds) [16]**, carved in alabaster, was purchased by Ede around 1968. The sculptor wrote that his work represented:

> *"birds alighting, or in flight or at take off ... it is really to do with freedom."*

Standing on the round table, Gaudier-Brzeska's **Dancer [15]** approaches movement in three dimensions in a different way. Originally modelled in plaster in mid-1913, the figure was a mature response to the sculptural notions of Auguste Rodin.

View of the dancer room

Rodin felt that movement in sculpture was best represented by showing the figure in transition from one pose to another. Gaudier-Brzeska captured precisely this moment as the dancer twists in space and steps down. The subtle hollows of this cast bronze version of the work are animated by the light, particularly around the torso. The sculptor continued these experiments in movement in later works, including *Red Stone Dancer* and *Wrestlers relief*, on display downstairs in the extension.

Another work, the marble **Mermaid [20]**, shows how, around 1913–14, Gaudier-Brzeska's technique was shifting from modelling in clay to direct carving in marble.

An example of the great care that Ede took in the placing of objects is the display around the semicircular table by the small window. Kenji Umeda's **Spirality [10]**, carved in white marble, is a softly contoured piece. The sculptor helped with the cleaning of the house in the late 1960s, and according to Ede, the work showed the influence of the artist's encounter with the works by Gaudier-Brzeska on that were displayed at Kettle's Yard. The organic forms of *Spirality* find a counterpoint in the linear clarity

of Lucie Rie's **Bowl (brown and white inlaid line) [9]**, positioned
next to it. The brightness of Umeda's marble is enhanced by
the juxtaposition with William Scott's subtle still life painting
Bowl (White on Grey) [11], hanging on the wall behind. Ede acquired
this work from the artist in exchange for an Alfred Wallis painting
in the early 1960s.

View of the house showing works by
Lucie Rie, Kenji Umeda and William Scott

Extension: Upstairs

Unknown
1   Javanese puppet, undated
    Mixed media

William Congdon
2   *Canal, Venice (Venice from the Giudecca)*, 1952
    Oil on hardboard

Unknown
3   Kurdistan embroidered trouser
    Textile

Ben Nicholson
4   *1930 (christmas night)*, 1930
    Oil and graphite on canvas

Henri Gaudier-Brzeska
5   *Madonna (Maria Carmi as the Madonna)*, 1912
    Painted plaster

Bryan Pearce
6   *King's College Chapel*, 1966
    Oil on hardboard

Ovidiu Maitec
7   *Radar II*, 1970
    Walnut wood

Ben Nicholson
8   *1927 may (still life with knife and lemon)*, 1927
    Oil on canvas

Barbara Hepworth
9   *Three Personages*, 1965
    Painted black slate on a wooden base

David Peace
10 *'While thus they sing …'*, c.1971
    Engraved glass

David Peace
11 *Sanctuary lamp*, 1955
    Engraved glass

Unknown
12 Bokhara Kelim, undated
    Textile

Simon Nicholson
13 *St Ives 12*, 1962
    Matches on strawboard

Winifred Nicholson
14 *Seascape with Dinghy*, c.1932
    Oil on canvas

Henri Gaudier-Brzeska
15 *Caritas*, 1914
    (posthumous cast, undated)
    Stone cast

Elisabeth Vellacott
16 *Entangled Trees*, 1976
    Graphite on paper

Winifred Nicholson
17 *Roman Road (Landscape with House and Barn)*, 1926
    Oil on canvas

William Congdon
18 *The Black City I (New York)*, 1949
    Oil, enamel and ink on hardboard

David Peace
19 *'CANST THOU BIND THE CLUSTER OF THE PLEIADES OR LOOSE THE BANDS OF ORION'*, 1961
    Engraved glass

Ben Nicholson
20 *1965 (goblet)*, 1965
    Pen and ink and wash on paper

Alberto Burri
21 *Buon*, c.1960
    Paint and collage on board

William Congdon
22 *India Temples no.1 (Sri Ranganathaswamy Temple, Tiruchirapalli)*, 1954
    Oil, gold paint and enamel on hardboard

Bryan Pearce
23 *The Round Church, Cambridge*, c.1966
    Oil on hardboard

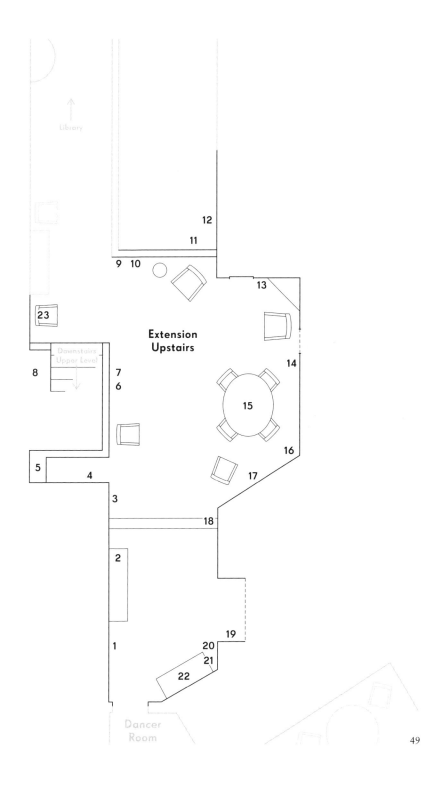

Library

12
11
9 10

13

23

Extension
Upstairs

14

Downstairs
Upper Level

8   7
           6

15

16

5

4   17

3

18

2

1   19

20

21

22

Dancer
Room

Extension: Library

Unknown
24 *Spanish glass*, late 18th Century

Alfred Wallis
25 *Fishes and lobster pots*, c. 1936
Oil on card

26 *Flowering trees*, undated
Oil on card

27 *Cottages in a wood –
St Ives*, c. 1935–37
Oil on card

28 *White house and cottages
(St. Ives)*, undated
Oil on card

29 *Lighthouse and two
sailing ships*, undated
Oil on card

30 *Boats before a great bridge
(Royal Albert Bridge)*, c. 1935–37
Oil on card

31 *St Michael's Mount*, undated
Oil on card

32 *Three-masted ship near
lighthouse*, 1928–30
Oil on board

33 *Penzance harbour*, undated
Oil on card

34 *Two boats*, undated
Oil on card

35 *P & O ship*, undated
Oil on card

36 *Seven boats entering
harbour*, 1925–26
Oil on card

37 *Schooner in full sail near
a lighthouse*, c. 1925–28
Oil on card

38 *Boats under Saltash Bridge
(Royal Albert Bridge)*, c. 1935–37
Oil on card

39 *Sailing ship and
orchard*, c. 1935–37
Oil on card

40 *Saltash (or Devonport)*,
c. 1928–30
Oil and watercolour on board

Brian Pearce
41 *St Ives Harbour*, undated
Oil on board

James Dixon
42 *Tory Island*, 1966
Oil and paper on board

Henri Gaudier-Brzeska
43 *Boy with uplifted arms*, 1913
(posthumous cast, 1968)
Bronze

Ben Nicholson
44 *head*, c. 1933
Linocut on card

45 *mug*, c. 1928
Linocut on card

46 *jug and bowl*, c. 1928
Linocut on card

Dorothy Stratford
47 *Jug*, 1959
Ceramic

Ben Nicholson
48 *abstract design*, 1934
Linocut on paper

Henri Gaudier-Brzeska
49 *Torso*, 1913
(posthumous cast, undated)
Bronze

Jan Ellison
50 *Red burnished
thumb pot*, c. 1957
Stoneware, glazed

Robin Welch
51 *Cylinder*, 1974
Ceramic

Zoë Ellison
52 *Vase*, c. 1955
Stoneware, glazed

Jirí Kolár
53 *Words in Music*, c. 1966
Collage, newspaper cuttings
on paper

Bernard Leach
54 *Bowl*, c. 1950
Stoneware, glazed

Katherine Pleydell-Bouverie
55 *Bowl*, 1974
Stoneware, glazed

56 *Bottle*, 1974
Stoneware, glazed

William Staite Murray
57 *Vase*, c. 1922
Earthenware, glazed

Henri Gaudier-Brzeska
58 *Wrestlers*, c. 1914
Graphite and brown wash
on paper

Christopher Wood
59 *Boy with Cat
(Jean Bourgoint)*, 1926
Oil and graphite on canvas

Alfred Wallis

60 *Trees and cottages*, c. 1935–37
Oil on card

Henri Gaudier-Brzeska

61 *Garden Ornament*, 1914
(posthumous cast, 1964)
Bronze

Alfred Wallis

62 *Land, fish and motor
vessel*, c. 1932–37
Oil on card

63 *Street of houses
and trees*, undated
Oil on card

64 *Two boats moving past
a big house*, c. 1932–37
Oil on card

65 *Ship, people and
animals*, undated
Oil on card

66 *Sailing ships and two steamers –
Newlyn harbour*, undated
Oil on board

67 *Harbour with two
lighthouses and motor vessel –
St Ives Bay*, c. 1932–34
Oil on card

68 *Mount's Bay with four
lighthouses*, undated
Oil, crayon and graphite
on card

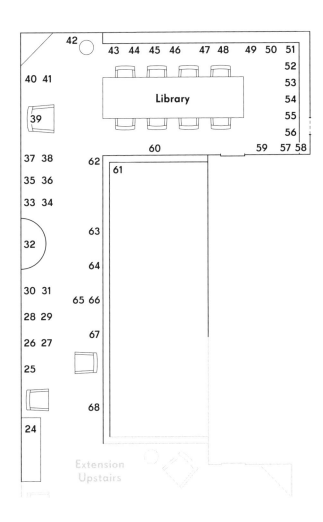

The physical and visual change from the cottages to the modern extension is introduced by a group of paintings by William Congdon. Congdon was born in the United States in 1912. After training as a sculptor, he served as an ambulance driver during the Second World War in Italy. At the end of the conflict he went back to the United States, where he turned to painting and was associated peripherally with Abstract Expressionism. In the late 1950s he moved to Italy, where he settled for the rest of his life. Jim Ede befriended Congdon by 1950, conducting an extensive correspondence and supporting the painter through his conversion to Roman Catholicism. Thanks to their friendship Ede amassed the most significant collection of works by Congdon in Britain.

The largest of these paintings, **India Temples no.1 (Sri Rangam Temples, Tiruchirapalli) [22]**, is representative of Congdon's technique, as he explained it in 1954:

*"Use a knife – never a brush which only compromises.
A knife constructs! – without tricks. Don't presume
to pick, mix, choose your colors, but toss a sea and fish
for gold in it. It comes with courage and freedom.
Don't mix colors – mix ideas, feelings."*

The artist travelled widely and encountered many different cultures. A second painting of the same temple hangs downstairs in the extension. The two images are very similar, suggesting that they were painted in quick succession. Like many of the artist's works at Kettle's Yard, they have a holy site as their central focus – here the golden temples rising from the lush forest, elsewhere Venetian churches or Istanbul's Hagia Sophia.

The strong visual impact of Congdon's works is counter-balanced by the small **Javanese puppet [1]**, placed in front of the mirror to the left of the door.

The text of David Peace's glass inscription, **CANST THOU BIND THE CLUSTER OF THE PLEIADES OR LOOSE THE BANDS OF ORION [19]** derives from the Book of Job. Peace drew on an eclectic range of sources for his inscriptions, and several other examples can be found throughout the house.

Works by Ben and Winifred Nicholson face one another in the area above the stairs. Ben Nicholson's **1930 (christmas night) [4]**, originally in the collection of Helen Sutherland, was a gift to Kettle's Yard from the collector Nicolete Gray in 1969, as was Winifred's **Roman Road (Landscape with House and Barn) [17]**. The latter is another example of the many paintings made in Cumbria after their return from Switzerland. Winifred's process

View of the upstairs
extension showing
Winifred Nicholson
*Roman Road (Landscape
with House and Barn)*, 1926

of painting directly from life meant that she worked quickly,
completing a canvas in a single sitting. At this time her subjects
were restricted geographically by the lack of transportation and
the weight of the materials. The size of this ambitious canvas
considerably exaggerated these problems. Winifred's practice,
which already ensured great speed of execution, is here stretched
to its limits. There is some evidence of preliminary composition
lines in the receding road, but large areas of canvas remain exposed
in the sky, and most are worked only cursorily. The broad areas
of colour are made all the more intense by Winifred's technique
of priming her canvases with white paint, before starting work.

Ben Nicholson's **1927 may (still life with knife and lemon) [8]**
was painted a year after *Roman Road (Landscape with Two
Houses)*. Although its technique parallels the quick handling in
Winifred's work, here the use of colour is much more concentrated.
This is particularly evident in the areas of intense red and blue.
The work shows Ben's developing awareness of the visual means
encountered in the work of the Parisian avant-garde, Braque
in particular.

The wooden carving **Radar II [7]**, by Romanian sculptor
Ovidiu Maitec, sits on a ledge in front of Nicholson's still
life. Maitec's reputation increased in the 1970s when he had
a number of shows in the UK including one at Kettle's Yard

in 1973. The title clearly derives from the Cold War era, but by carving in wood and allowing the natural patterns of the material to show, the sculptor relates this modern subject to Romanian folk art traditions. Maitec's work was viewed by many as continuing a wood-carving tradition established by Brancusi. The placing of the piece again exploits the lighting conditions at Kettle's Yard to the full.

At floor level under Maitec's carving hangs Bryan Pearce's **King's College Chapel [6]**. Pearce was born in 1929 at St Ives and in spite of suffering from phenylketonuria, a rare genetic disorder that requires round-the-clock care, he successfully attended the local school of art. His paintings at Kettle's Yard are very representative of his work as a whole: their focus is on the detail of ships and buildings. *King's College Chapel* and **The Round Church, Cambridge [23]** were painted after a trip to see Jim Ede at Kettle's Yard.

Library Extension

Walking through to the library, we encounter a comprehensive display of paintings by Alfred Wallis. The aspect of Wallis that most delighted Jim Ede was the directness and simplicity of his language, unmediated by any formal training. Drawing on his experience as a fisherman and usually working from memory, Wallis was able to translate into images his extraordinary

View leading to the library showing paintings by Alfred Wallis

knowledge of the sea and the Cornish coastline with great accuracy. Ede bought these paintings directly from the artist, who would send batches in the post to Ede's Hampstead home in the late 1920s and throughout the 1930s.

Wallis did not adopt the conventional one-point perspective of academic painting. This allows the viewer to experience the scene more directly, by standing amongst the boats and the harbour rather than before them. A good example is **St Michael's Mount [31]**, where the distortion of perspective and scale is particularly apparent. Wallis was happy to make use of whatever material came to hand: he often painted on cardboard, given to him by the local grocer, and used industrially produced boat paint. **Boats before a great bridge [30]**, for instance, shows Wallis' liking for the use of irregularly shaped supports. In **Three-masted ship near a lighthouse [32]** the uneven use of paint allows the board manufacturer's stamp to be clearly seen at the top of the image. These aspects of Wallis' art show an unawareness of artistic conventions which made his work particularly appealing to painters such as Ben Nicholson and Christopher Wood, at a time when they were attempting to break with tradition and working towards the creation of new pictorial languages.

Parallels can be drawn between Wallis' work and that of James Dixon, whose **Tory Island [42]** hangs to the left of the library. Like the Cornish painter, Dixon was a fisherman and painted with the knowledge of a local working man. He lived for his entire life on Tory Island, off the Donegal Coast (Ireland), and took up painting in the last years of his life, encouraged to do so by the painter Derek Hill. His works show the rhythms of the seasons and the dramatic climatic conditions of his native land.

At the other end of the library hangs Christopher Wood's **Boy with Cat (Jean Bourgoint) [59]**. The model for this portrait was Jean Bourgoint, a Parisian friend of Wood's who, together with his sister Jeanne, had inspired Cocteau's novel of sibling love and destruction *Les Enfants Terribles*.

Above the bookshelves is Ben Nicholson's linocut print **head [44]**, a stark black and white profile portrait of Barbara Hepworth. Executed during a trip to France, the work is a tender testament to the developing relationship between the two artists after Nicholson's separation from Winifred. An example of Barbara Hepworth's work can be found walking back towards the stairs, where her black slate sculpture *Three Personages* is on display. The work shows the artist's engagement with the pre-historic quoits and standing stones of the Penwith peninsula, which had captivated her since her arrival in St Ives in 1939.

Extension: Downstairs Upper Level

David Jones
1   *Quia per Incarnati*, c. 1953
    Watercolour and graphite
    on paper

William Scott
2   *Message Obscure I*, 1965
    Oil on canvas

Georges Braque
3   *Le Cygne Volant*, c. late 1950s
    Lithograph on paper

Kate Nicholson
4   *Skye*, 1949
    Oil on canvas

Henri Gaudier-Brzeska
5   *Seated Woman*, 1914
    (posthumous cast, 1964)
    Bronze

Christopher Wood
6   *Building the Boat,*
    Tréboul, 1930
    Oil on board

Ben Nicholson
7   *1927 (snowscape)*, 1927
    Oil on canvas

Henri Gaudier-Brzeska
8   *Bird Swallowing a Fish*, 1914
    Painted plaster

Ben Nicholson
9   *1955 (spello)*, 1955
    Graphite and watercolour
    on card

Christopher Wood
10 *Landscape at Vence –*
    Little White House, 1927
    Oil on canvas

Henri Gaudier-Brzeska
11 *Birds Erect*, 1914
    (posthumous cast, undated)
    Stone cast

Lucie Rie
12 *Bowl*, c. 1971–74
    Ceramic

Laurence Stephen Lowry
13 *Mountain Lake*, 1943
    Oil on board

Henri Gaudier-Brzeska
14 *Head of Mlle Borne*, 1914
    (posthumous cast, undated)
    Bronze

Winifred Nicholson
15 *Cyclamen and Primula*, c. 1923
    Oil on board

16 *Seascape (Sea and Sand)*, 1926
    Oil on canvas

17 *Sam Graves*, c. 1930
    Oil on board

Henri Gaudier-Brzeska
18 *Three Monkeys*, 1914
    Sandstone

Italo Valenti
19 *Nr. 345; La Tua Ombra;*
    Ton Ombre, 1966
    Paper collage on paper

20 *Nr. 380; Trinome*, 1966
    Paper collage on card

Eric Gill
21 *My First Inscription*
    (Jane Lister), c. 1903
    Marble

Kenneth Martin
22 *Screw mobile*, 1969
    Brass

Italo Valenti
23 *Nr. 318; Troll II*, 1964
    Paper collage on board

24 *Nr. 222; Zillis*, 1963–70
    Paper collage on paper

Henry Moore
25 *Sculptural Object*, 1960
    Bronze on limestone base

Italo Valenti
26 *Nr. 81; Pierres de*
    Lune, 1960–69
    Paper and collage
    on painted board

Italo Valenti
27 *Nr. 121; Orlanda*, 1968
    Oil on canvas

28 *Nr. 145; Languana;*
    Lagune, 1968
    Oil on canvas

Bryan Pearce
29 *The Queen Mary*, undated
    Oil on hardboard

John Catto
30 *St. Edmund*, found object,
    given to Ede in 1975
    Charred willow wood

David Peace
31 *Glass carboy, 'And a*
    river went out …', 1970
    Engraved glass

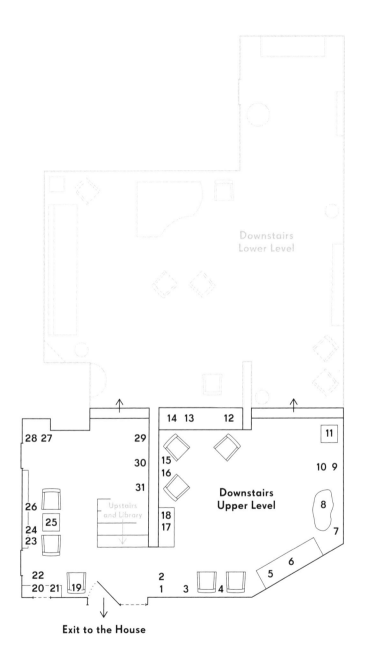

Downstairs
Lower Level

14 13   12

11

28 27   29

15

16   Downstairs
                         Upper Level   10 9

30

31   8

26   7

25   Upstairs
            and Library

24   18
23   17

22

20 21   19   2
                     1   3   4   5   6

Exit to the House

At the foot of the stairs we encounter David Jones' coloured inscription, **Quia per Incarnati [1]**, partly taken from the Christmas Preface to the Mass. Translated, the inscription reads:

> *"For by the mystery of the Word made flesh the light of thy brightness has shone anew into the eyes of our mind. Minerva has sprung from the head of Jove".*

The clarity of the lettering and the use of appealing gold, green and red contrast with the way in which the words run into one another, making the reading difficult. This seems to be Jones' way of inviting the viewer to slow down and engage with the intellectual and spiritual content of the text.

To the left of the inscription is Gaudier-Brzeska's **Seated Woman [5]**. Like **Birds Erect [11]** and **Bird Swallowing a Fish [8]**, on its left, this piece was completed in 1914, just before the sculptor's departure for the trenches.

Although by this time Gaudier-Brzeska was committed to the technique of direct carving, lack of money often forced him to use whatever material was available. In *Bird Swallowing a Fish*, for instance, he modelled plaster and painted it green to make it resemble bronze. The subject derived from an incident observed by the sculptor in Hyde Park. Made at the climax of Gaudier-Brzeska's engagement with Vorticism, this work represents an attempt to portray organic forms in a rigidly symmetrical and almost mechanical way. The tension and air of menace are unmistakable: several have commented on the fish's likeness to a bomb.

Birds Erect bears a closer relationship with contemporary French Cubist sculpture. Its angular, block-like masses make it Gaudier-Brzeska's most abstract statement. A preparatory drawing again indicates that the subject derives from one of the sculptor's sketching trips in the parks of London.

Above the side-board hangs Christopher Wood's **Building the Boat, Tréboul [6]**. This was one of the artist's last paintings before his untimely death in August 1930. Completed in Brittany, the work carefully describes the local architecture and the costume worn by the women. Wood's interest in the work of Paul Gauguin, Vincent Van Gogh and Alfred Wallis is noticeable in the maritime subject, the rough handling of paint and a colour range of non-naturalistic greens and blue-greys.

Three works by Winifred Nicholson are grouped on the wall opposite. **Sam Graves [17]** is a portrait of the youngest son of the novelist Robert Graves and his wife Nancy, sister of Ben Nicholson.

The vigorous brushwork around the child's pink shirt and blond curls gives a good indication of the vivacity and immediacy of Winifred's technique. **Seascape (Sea and Sand) [16]** was painted during a holiday that the Edes and the Nicholsons took together at a house rented by Helen Sutherland at Bamburgh, on the Northumberland coast. Ede remembered that the work was painted outdoors, in windy and wet conditions. The artist completed it with great difficulty, with the painting being blown onto her clothes on several occasions. The heavy working of the incoming waves conveys a sense of these conditions. **Cyclamen and Primula [15]** is one in a series of still lifes with flowers wrapped in paper and set against a landscape painted in the early 1920s, in Italian Switzerland. Talking of these paintings, Winifred Nicholson remembered that:

> *"Ben had given me a pot of lilies of the valley – mughetti – in a tissue paper wrapper – this I stood on the window sill – behind was the azure blue, Mountain, Lake, Sky, all there – and the tissue paper wrapper held the secret of the universe. That picture painted itself, and after that the same theme painted itself on that window sill, in cyclamen, primula or cineraria – sunlight on leaves, and sunlight shining transparent through lens and through the mystery of tissue paper … I have often wished for another painting spell like that, but never had one."*

Returning to the foot of the staircase, we encounter Georges Braque's print **Le Cygne Volant [3]**. The lithograph was probably acquired by Ede during his residence in France, between 1952 and 1956. Jim had known Braque since the 1930s, when the artist visited his house in Hampstead.

Against the background of Italo Valenti's abstract works stands Henry Moore's **Sculptural Object [25]**. The piece shows an interesting contrast with the *Head* in Jim Ede's bedroom, revealing changes in conception, technique and material in the artist's work over a period of thirty-five years.

The burnt wood **St Edmund [30]**, under the stairs, is a remarkable object. This is a piece of charred willow found by John Catto, a friend of Ede's, by the River Cam. He presented the piece to Kettle's Yard in 1975. Jim named the piece St Edmund, as it reminded him of medieval carvings of the saint.

View of the extension
above the slate

Extension: Downstairs Lower Level

Henri Gaudier-Brzeska
1 *Female Torso*, 1913
(posthumous cast, 1976)
Resin cast

William Congdon
2 *Sri Rangam Temple,
Tiruchirapalli (Sri Rangam,
Tiruchirapalli)*, 1954
Oil, gold paint and enamel
on hardboard

Constantin Brancusi
3 *Golden Fish*, 1924
(posthumous cast, 1969)
Brass and steel

Gregorio Vardenega
4 *Small Sphere*, c.1956
Plexiglass

Henri Gaudier-Brzeska
5 *Head*, c.1912
Ceramic

6 *Figure*, 1914
Alabaster

William Staite Murray
7 *Vase*, c.1930
Terracotta, glazed

8 *Vase*, c.1930
Terracotta, glazed

Christopher Wood
9 *Ulysses and the Siren
(Mermaids)*, 1929
Oil on hardboard

George Kennethson
10 *Forms*, c.1968
Staffordshire alabaster

Ben Nicholson
11 *1933 (musical instruments)*, 1933
Oil on canvas

Naum Gabo
12 *Linear Construction
in Space No.1*, 1944–45
Perspex and nylon thread

Henri Gaudier-Brzeska
13 *Wrestlers relief*, 1913
(posthumous cast, 1965)
Herculite cast

Naum Gabo
14 *Opus 5
(The Constellations)*, 1950
Monoprint on paper

Marino Marini
15 *Rider on a Horse*, c.1957
Etching and Indian ink wash
on paper

Henri Gaudier-Brzeska
16 *Two Men with a Bowl*, 1913–14
(posthumous cast c.1965)
Bronze cast

Ben Nicholson
17 *princess (kings and
queens)*, c.1933
Linocut on cloth

Henri Gaudier-Brzeska
18 *Seated Fawn*, 1913
(posthumous cast, 1920s)
Bronze

Ben Nicholson
19 *two mugs*, 1928–29
Linocut on paper

Cecil Collins
20 *The Years*, 1937
Pen and ink and wash
on paper

Bryan Illsley
21 *White Relief*, 1966
White cardboard on paper

Ben Nicholson
22 *jug and two mugs*, c.1928
Linocut on paper

Henri Gaudier-Brzeska
23 *Horace Brodzky Mask*, 1913
Stone

John Clegg
24 *Fiddle Fish*, 1963
Marble and string

Italo Valenti
25 *Nr. 284; Etana*, 1964
Paper collage on hardboard

26 *Nr. 287; Giardino
a mezzogiorno;
Jardin a midi*, 1964
Paper collage on hardboard

27 *Nr. 286; Pietra; Pierre*, 1964
Paper collage on hardboard

Lucie Rie
28 *Conical Bowl*, 1971
Stoneware bowl, glazed

Frank Auerbach
29 *R.B. Kitaj*, 1980
Etching on paper

Ben Nicholson
30 *1934 (abstract design)*, 1934
Linocut on paper

31 *1933 (profiles)*, 1933
Linocut on paper

Christopher Wood
32 *Self Portrait*, 1927
Oil on canvas

Roger Hilton
33 *January 1961 (Black and
Brown on White)*, 1961
Oil on canvas

Edmond Xavier Kapp
34 *Design*, 1965
   Grey wash on paper

Italo Valenti
35 *Veneti*, 1964
   Paper collage on board

Ben Nicholson
36 *1928 (three mugs and
   a bowl)*, 1928
   Linocut on paper

Unknown
37 *Khmer Buddha*,
   c. 13–14th Century
   Stone

Mario Sironi
38 *Drawing for reliefs
   (six half-length figures)*, c. 1940s
   Conté crayon and charcoal
   on paper

Henri Gaudier-Brzeska
39 *Woman and Dog*, 1914
   Charcoal on paper

40 *Garden Ornament*, 1914
   Bronze

Ben Nicholson
41 *1924 (goblet and
   two pears)*, 1924
   Oil and graphite on board

42 *1930 (plate, cup and jug)*, 1930
   Oil and graphite on board

43 *1962 (Argos)*, 1962
   Oil and carved board on wood

44 *1924 (Bertha no. 2)*, 1924
   Oil and graphite on canvas

Henri Gaudier-Brzeska
45 *Maternity (Mother and Child)*,
   1913 (posthumous cast, 1960s)
   Bronze cast

46 *Lady Macbeth poster*, 1912
   Gouache on paper

Ben Nicholson
47 *1924 June (Balearic Isles)*, 1924
   Oil and graphite on canvas

48 *exhibition sign*, c. 1933
   Oil on linoleum

Henri Gaudier-Brzeska
49 *Red Stone Dancer*, 1913–14
   (posthumous cast, 1969)
   Bronze

Ben Nicholson
50 *Porta – San Gimingnano*, 1953
   Etching on paper

Winston MacQuoid
51 *Waterfall in the Glen*, 1927
   Oil on plywood

Alfred Wallis
52 *Old Arch Digey
   (St. Ives)*, undated
   Oil on card (verso-graphite)

Henri Gaudier-Brzeska
53 *Woman Carrying Sacks*, 1912–13,
   (posthumous cast, 1964)
   Bronze

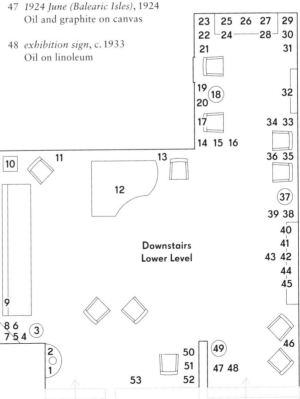

Downstairs
Lower Level

View of the extension
showing the piano and
works by Ben Nicholson
and George Kennethson

The extension is frequently used for musical recitals. Jim Ede
viewed music as an essential component of Kettle's Yard.
The special combination of natural light, carefully designed
space, music and works of art can all be enjoyed during the many
concerts that still take place at Kettle's Yard.

A musical theme is emphasised by the placement of Ben
Nicholson's **1933 (musical instruments) [11]** to the left of the grand
piano. Rhythm is a central feature of this work, both in the
arrangement of the guitars and in the sweeping linear incisions
on the paint surface. Nicholson's restricted palette, of red set
against browns and greys, and the complex spatial arrangement
of the piece again show a response to the 1920s still lifes of
Georges Braque. The work was painted shortly before Nicholson
made his first reliefs and entered the realm of pure abstraction.

On the Steinway piano sits one of two constructions
by the Russian-born sculptor Naum Gabo, **Linear Construction
in Space No. 1 [12]** or *Construction in Space: Suspended*, 1962.
Appropriately, rhythm is again central to both works, which
are alternated on display due to their fragility. Each construction
sets up an engaging series of conversations – with itself and its

surroundings – between solidity and lightness, mass and void, movement and stillness, transparency and density. Gabo was one of the the first sculptors to work with Perspex: in these pieces he used the newly invented material to create structures around which he stretched thin nylon filaments. His vision that art should contribute to social improvement ties in well with the type of experience that Ede wanted to offer at Kettle's Yard. The artist, who had repeatedly visited Jim in his London home, thus expressed his view in 1944:

> "I think that the image my work invokes is the image
> of good – not of evil; the image of order – not of chaos;
> the image of life – not of death. And that is all the
> content of my constructions amounts to. I should think
> that this is equally all that the constructive idea is
> driving at."

Evidence of Ede's friendship with Gabo can be found in the affectionate dedication of the monoprint **Opus 5 (The Constellations) [14]** displayed around the corner.

At the far end of this area hang three collages by Italo Valenti: **Nr. 284; Etana [25]**, **Nr. 287; Giardino a mezzogiorno; Jardin a midi [26]**, and **Nr. 286; Pietra; Pierre [27]**, all acquired from the Documenta III exhibition in 1964. Placed under a skylight and behind the slate table, the works assume an almost devotional character, like a triptych above an altar. Ben Nicholson had introduced Ede to Valenti's art, and soon a firm friendship between Jim and the Italian artist developed. This episode is again testament to Nicholson's enduring influence on Ede's taste. Ede remembered the impact that the works had on him:

> "My introduction to these collage works was a tremendous
> event ... Black really became black, and white had infinite
> variety. The skill and sensibility with which these pieces
> of paper were torn, left me amazed."

On the slate table under the collages, a carefully selected group of objects – including John Clegg's **Fiddle Fish [24]** and Lucie Rie's **Conical Bowl [28]**, which was often referred to at Kettle's Yard as *The Wave* – enhances the altar-like appearance and establishes an arresting dialogue with the Valentis. Moreover, the juxtaposition of Lucie Rie's bowl with the Cypriot jug on the floor, dating from c.700 B.C., offers an interesting interplay of light and dark, ancient and modern.

A more worldly presence is suggested by Christopher Wood's **Self Portrait [32]**, although the curious disproportion of the head and hands gives the painting an almost hieratical appearance. The sense of mystery and transcendence is enhanced by the depiction of the artist's eyes exactly on the line of the horizon, and in the same colour as the sky. Wood portrayed himself with a paintbrush in hand, seated next to his palette, hemmed in by the Paris cityscape behind him. The artist meets our gaze confidently and self-consciously shows himself as a painter at the height of his powers, living in the capital of the Western avant-garde. As is often the case with large self portraits, this was possibly intended as a major statement. Wood was at the time in the process of establishing a personal style and hoped to make his London reputation through his contribution to the Beaux Arts Gallery show in which the painting was included.

Christopher Wood, *Self Portrait*, 1927

Opposite
View of the downstairs extension

Two Buddhas – one amongst the plates in the dresser by the long couch, the other resting on three wooden columns opposite the piano – again show Ede's interest in Eastern cultures. The larger **Buddha [37]** is Khmer, or Cambodian, and dates from the thirteenth or fourteenth century.

The work of Gaudier-Brzeska is as important to the extension as it is elsewhere in the house. Here **Two Men with a Bowl [16]** gives clear evidence of Gaudier-Brzeska's interest in African art, whereas the enlarged forms of the nose and ears of the **Horace Brodzky Mask [23]** – on the floor under the Valentis – show his more playful, satirical side.

The display, above the long wooden table, of a group of Ben Nicholson's paintings dating from different periods of his career represents a fascinating attempt to summarise his artistic development between the 1920s and 1950s. One work in particular, **1962 (Argos) [42]**, with its geometrical construction, engages in a stimulating dialogue with the architecture of the extension.

Biographical Notes

John Acland (b.c.1940) studied at Magdalene College, Cambridge, in the late 1950s and regularly visited Kettle's Yard. His slate sculpture was carved in Cornwall.

Jane Adams (b.1949) is Jim Ede's granddaughter.

Frank Auerbach (b.1931) was born in Berlin. In 1939 he was sent to England to escape Nazism. During the 1950s he attended St Martin's School of Art and the Royal College of Art in London. In 1986 he represented Britain at the Venice Biennale.

John Blackburn (b.1935) trained at the Maidenhead School of Art. After spending seven years in New Zealand, he settled near Canterbury. His work of the 1960s is in an abstract style close to that of Hilton, Pasmore and Scott.

Constantin Brancusi (1876–1957) was born in Hobitza, Romania. In 1904 he moved to Paris, where he spent the rest of his life. In Paris, under Rodin's influence, he gradually evolved a pure, abstract manner that strove to depict the formal essence of objects without rejecting the natural world.

Georges Braque (1882–1963) was born in Argenteuil, near Paris. By 1909 his close collaboration with Picasso had led to the evolution of a revolutionary approach to painting, subsequently called Cubism. After the First World War, Braque returned to more naturalistic still life and figure compositions, aiming at a perfect balance and harmony between colour and design.

John Clegg (b.1935) was born in Nottingham. After studying at the Leys School and Magdalene College in Cambridge, he worked as an archaeologist and lectured at Brisbane University, Australia. In addition to his work as a sculptor, he developed an interest in aboriginal art.

Cecil Collins (1908–89) was born in Plymouth. He studied at the local School of Art (1924–27) and the Royal College of Art (1927–31). Influenced by Blake, Chagall and the Surrealists (two of his works were included in the 1936 'International Surrealist Exhibition' at the Burlington Galleries, London), his visionary art was concerned with religious and spiritual inquiry.

William Congdon (1912–98) was born at Rhode Island, USA, and studied at the Pennsylvania Academy of Fine Arts. After serving as an ambulance driver during the war, he settled in Italy and converted to Catholicism in 1959. He lived in Assisi (Italy) in the 1960s and 1970s, painting a series of pictures of Venice and Subiaco. From 1979 he lived in Gudo Gambaredo, near Milan.

Francine Del Pierre (1917–71) French potter, exhibited with Bernard Leach in Japan. She opened a studio in Vence with Albert Diato. All of her work is coiled and in earthenware.

James Dixon (1887–1970) was born on Tory Island, off the west coast of Ireland, where he spent his life working as a crofter and fisherman. He took up painting when encouraged to do so by an artist visiting the island, Derek Hill.

Zoë Ellison (d.1977) was trained at the Ewenny Pottery, Glamorgan and Camberwell College of Art. She taught at the Cambridge School of Art and, with husband Jan, set up the Cross Keys Pottery in Cambridge.

Max Ernst (1891–1976) was born in Brühl, near Cologne, Germany. After studying philosophy in Bonn, in 1913 he went to Paris, where he met many of the leading avant-garde artists. Ernst was instrumental to the development of Surrealism in Germany. He helped to organise the first Surrealist exhibition in Paris in 1925. During the Second World War he emigrated to America.

Ian Hamilton Finlay (1925–2006) was born in Nassau, Bahamas. He went to art school in Glasgow before joining the army. He published many different kinds of visual and concrete poems through his own magazine Poor. Old. Tired. Horse. At his home in Lanarkshire, he created a garden filled with sculptural and landscape versions of his pastoral and militarist imagery. Finlay often acknowledged the influence of Kettle's Yard in his work.

Naum Gabo (1890–1977) was born in Bryansk, Russia. In 1921 he moved to Berlin where he and his brother, Antoine Pevsner, became leading exponents of Constructivist art. In 1933 he moved to London, where he worked with Ben Nicholson and Leslie Martin, both of whom shared his interest in the concepts of purity and structure. Together they edited the book Circle in 1937. He went to St Ives with Nicholson during the war, and then emigrated to America, where he spent the rest of his life.

Henri Gaudier-Brzeska (1891–1915) was born in St Jean de Braye, near Orléans, in France. He met Sophie Brzeska while working as a student at Ste. Geneviève Library in Paris in 1910. In the same year he left France under a cloud of social hostility and settled in England assuming the name of Brzeska soon after. He worked in isolation in London until he met Middleton Murry in 1912, whereafter he built up a circle of colleagues which included Ezra Pound, Wyndham Lewis and T. E. Hulme. He became involved in Pound's and Lewis' Vorticist group, contributing to the two issues of their magazine BLAST. He was killed in action during the First World War.

Eric Gill (1882–1940) was born in Brighton. He took up inscription work in 1903. He ran the St Dominic's Press from Ditchling, Sussex, where he lived for a time with David Jones, who followed him to his second community of artists and craftsmen at Capel-y-Ffin in Wales. Gill designed many typefaces, two of which are still in common use, Monotype Perpetua and Gill Sans. He was well respected for his sculpture and lithography, and produced illustrations for editions of the Four Gospels and of The Canterbury Tales.

Barbara Hepworth (1903–75) was born in Wakefield, Yorkshire. In the early 1920s she was a student at Leeds School of Art and the Royal College of Art. In 1931 she met Ben Nicholson, who was to become her second husband seven years later. She took part in various group exhibitions in the 1930s, including those of Abstraction-Création, the Seven & Five Society and Unit One. She contributed to Circle in 1937. Hepworth lived in Cornwall from 1939 until her death, caused by a fire in her studio.

Roger Hilton (1911–75) studied at the Slade School of Art, London, between 1929 and 1931 and later at the Académie Ranson in Paris. He became a leading figure of British Abstract painting. In 1965 he settled in St Ives after visiting Patrick Heron. His work since the war has been mainly associated with the Cornish School, maintaining a balance between the figurative and the abstract.

Bryan Illsley (b. 1937) lives in St Ives, Cornwall. A painter and jewellery maker, he has worked with the Leach Pottery.

David Jones (1895–1974) was born in Brockley, South London, the son of a Welsh printer. He studied at the Camberwell School of Art before the First World War. He was associated with Eric Gill's communities of artists and craftsmen in Sussex and Wales in the 1920s, working as an engraver and printer, while at the same time writing poetry and essays. His work reflects his interest in early Christianity, Arthurian myths and the ancient classical world.

Edmond Xavier Kapp (1890–1978) was an official war artist (1940–41) and artist to UNESCO (1946–47). He is the only painter to have had Picasso sit for a portrait.

George Kennethson (1910–94) was born in Richmond, Surrey. After attending the Royal College of Art (1928–32), he exhibited regularly in London and Cambridge. From the mid-1950s he lived and taught at Oundle.

Simon Kenrick (b. 1943) studied architecture and history of art at Cambridge. He has subsequently worked as an architect.

Jirí Kolár (1914–2002) was born in Protivín, Bohemia. He began his career as a poet. In the 1950s his poems began to reach out to the visual realm in a variety of media. In the 1960s he explored geometrical abstraction, visual poems and three-dimensional objects. Kolár is most famous for his collages and innovative art techniques, including chiasmages, rollages and wrinklages.

Bernard Leach (1887–1979) was born in Hong Kong to British parents and grew up in Japan. At the age of ten he moved to Great Britain. In 1909 he returned to Japan where he worked as an etcher. Having decided to turn to pottery, he moved back to England. In 1920 he set up the Leach Pottery in St Ives with Shoji Hamada. Initially his works were influenced by Oriental traditions, but gradually he drew upon a wider range of sources including English slipware, medieval pots and tiles, Minoan and pre-Columbian work.

Laurence Stephen Lowry (1887–1976) was born in Manchester. He is best known for his paintings of northern industrial cities, expressing a sense of alienation. He occasionally painted views of the Lake District, such as the picture in Kettle's Yard.

Ovidiu Maitec (1925–2006) was born in Romania. He was Vice-President of the Romanian artists union, and exhibited in many galleries outside his native country. He carved in walnut, creating hinged or rotating works which reflect the Romanian tradition of woodcarving.

Marino Marini (1901–80) was born in Pistoia, near Florence. A member of the Novecento group in the 1930s, he built up his international reputation with sculptures of animals and riders on horses. He was also a painter, lithographer and etcher.

Kenneth Martin (1905–84) was born in Sheffield. He studied at the Sheffield School of Art and the Royal College of Art, London. In 1930 he married the artist Mary Balmford: they rarely worked in collaboration but occasionally exhibited together. Martin's work was exhibited at the Tate Gallery (1975) and Kettle's Yard (1999).

Winston McQuoid (b.1909–84) was born in Glasgow. He attended art schools in Belfast, Nantwich and London. His first solo show was held in Belfast in 1924, when he was only 14. He was a well-known portrait artist from the 1930s (his sitters included Osbert Sitwell). In 1969 he moved to Ireland.

Joan Miró (1893–1983) was born in Barcelona, Spain. Between the wars he worked in Paris, where he associated with Picasso and the Surrealists. For a short time his art showed the influence of the advanced movements in European painting, but he soon developed his own personal language of signs and symbols, painting pictures deeply rooted in his Catalan heritage.

Henry Moore (1898–1986) was born in Castleford, Yorkshire. In the early 1920s he was influenced by Gaudier-Brzeska and primitive art. During the following decade he was a member of the Seven & Five Society and Unit One, and helped found the British Surrealist movement in 1936. He was an official war artist during the Second World War. A sculptor of major international reputation, he gained many public commissions. His works, whether carved or modelled, show an awareness of natural forms.

Ben Nicholson (1894–1982) was the son of the painter William Nicholson. He married Winifred Roberts and travelled widely with her between Cumberland, London, Paris and Switzerland in the 1920s. Nicholson developed a consciously primitive landscape style in 1927, further encouraged by his encounter with the art of Alfred Wallis. Between 1931 and 1939 he lived in London and met artists and critics such as Moore, Piper, Martin, Ede, Herbert Read and Barbara Hepworth (who became his second wife in 1938). He also met Arp, Brancusi, and later Mondrian, Gabo and Jean Hélion in Paris. Nicholson developed a highly abstract style in the late 1930s. He returned to St Ives during the war and established an international reputation in the 1950s and 60s. After the war he lived at various times in London, Cambridge and Switzerland.

Kate Nicholson (b.1929) is the daughter of Ben and Winifred Nicholson.

Simon Nicholson (1934–90) was the son of Ben Nicholson and Barbara Hepworth.

Winifred Nicholson (1893–1981) was born in Oxford. She studied in London before marrying Ben Nicholson in 1920. She exhibited with her husband in the 1920s and was a member of the Seven & Five Society between 1925 and 1935. In 1937 she contributed to Circle under the name of Dacre. After the war she settled in Cumberland.

Roger Oates (b.1941) was born in Yorkshire. He works as a textile designer and has exhibited throughout Britain.

David Peace (1915–2003) lived and worked near Cambridge. His glass engravings are to be found in many collections, including the Victoria and Albert Museum. He was the first chairman of the Guild of Glass Engravers.

Bryan Pearce (1929–2007) was born in St Ives. In spite of suffering from phenylketonuria, he successfully attended the local school of art. His paintings focus on the detail of ships and buildings.

Michael Pine (b.1935) is an architect. He lived in St Ives for many years and now lives and works in Canada.

John Piper (1903–92) was born in Epsom, Surrey. An abstract artist in the 1930s, he later developed a more representational style. One of the most versatile British artists of the 20th century, he is also known for his theatre sets and stained glass designs.

Katherine Pleydell-Bouverie (1895–1985) became interested in ceramics after seeing pots by Roger Fry, and enrolled in classes at the Central School of Arts and Crafts, London. In 1924 she became one of

Bernard Leach's first students in St Ives. After a year there, she started her own workshop, the Cole Pottery, in Berkshire. She became well known for her work with ash glazes. After the Second World War she moved to Warminster, Wiltshire.

Richard Pousette-Dart (1916–92) was born in Minnesota. The son of a painter and a poet and musician, he was largely self-taught. During the 1940s he became associated with Abstract Expressionism. He worked with sculpture, painting and photography, and taught at various institutions, including Columbia University.

Lucie Rie (1902–95) was born in Vienna, Austria. After training at the KunstgewerbeSchule, she moved to England in 1938. She worked with Hans Coper for many years, but it was only in the 1950s that the quality of her work was recognised. She taught at Camberwell College.

William Scott (1913–89) was born in Greenock, Scotland. After training at the Belfast School of Art, in 1932 he moved to London to study at the Royal Academy. While in the city, he became associated with Abstract Expressionism. After war service he moved to Somerset, but kept in touch with those artists who were developing an abstract style in St Ives, notably Heron, Lanyon and Hilton. From the mid-1950s he received many large-scale commissions.

Mario Sironi (1885–1961) was born in Sassari, Sardinia. He studied in Rome and through Boccioni came into contact with the Futurists. He was later influenced by the Pittura Metafisica movement. A founder member of the Novecento group in 1922, he painted numerous frescoes, including those for the University of Rome.

William Staite Murray (1881–1962) trained at the Camberwell College of Art. He taught pottery at the Royal College of Art between 1926 and 1940, and was a member of the Seven & Five Society.

Kenji Umeda (b. 1948) was born in Japan. While studying in Cambridge, in the early 1960s he helped Jim Ede with the cleaning of Kettle's Yard. After working as a painter, he became interested in sculpture, following a visit to Carrara, the home of marble.

Italo Valenti (1912–95) was born in Milan. He lived and worked in Italy until 1953, when he made his home in Switzerland. In 1963 he held a joint exhibition with Ben Nicholson, Mark Tobey, Jean Arp and Jules Bissier. He was introduced to Jim Ede by Ben Nicholson.

Gregorio Vardanega (b. 1923) was born near Venice. He studied in South America and was a member of the Art Concret group. After exhibiting in Europe in the 1950s and meeting artists such as Brancusi, Pevsner and Sonia Delaunay, he settled in Paris.

Elisabeth Vellacott (1905–2002) attended the Royal College of Art between 1925 and 1929. At the beginning of her career she worked as a textile and theatrical designer. After the war she moved away from design to concentrate on drawing and painting. She was a founder member of the Cambridge Society of Painters and Sculptors in 1954. She exhibited regularly in London and held retrospective exhibitions at Kettle's Yard in 1981 and 1995.

Alfred Wallis (1855–1942) was born in Devon. He was a fisherman and later a scrap-metal merchant in St Ives. After the death of his wife in 1922 he turned to painting. He was admired by Ben Nicholson and Christopher Wood, who came across him when visiting St Ives in 1928, and who included his work in the Seven & Five Society's exhibition of 1929. He died in Madron Poorhouse.

Robin Welch (b. 1936) studied at Penzance School of Art and the Central School of Arts and Crafts, London. He worked part-time at the Leach Pottery between 1953 and 1959 before opening his own workshop in London in 1960, which ran for two years. Welch opened another workshop in Eye, Suffolk in 1965.

Laurence Whistler (1912–2000) was a celebrated glass engraver, who also published a number of books on his own work as well as collections of poetry and essays on architecture.

Christopher Wood (1901–30) was born in Liverpool. Through extended visits to Paris between 1921 and 1924 he came into contact with avant-garde artists like Picasso and Jean Cocteau. In Britain he became close friends with Ben and Winifred Nicholson, painting with them in Cumberland in 1928. That year he also met Alfred Wallis on a visit to St Ives with Ben Nicholson. He first visited Brittany in 1929, returning in 1930. He was under the influence of opium when he was killed by a train at Salisbury station.

This edition of the Kettle's Yard House Guide in 2018 is edited by
Jennifer Powell. With thanks to Andrew Nairne, Frieda Midgley
and Amy Tobin. Published by Kettle's Yard, University of Cambridge.

The 2018 edition has been revised to include new sections on
Kettle's Yard Today, Helen Ede's Bedroom and the Attic as well as
a new selection of colour images. The majority of the core texts that
accompany each room of the house are taken from the 2002 edition
of the House Guide which was written by Sebastiano Barassi,
assisted by Jonathan Blackwood.

We would like to thank the Friends of Kettle's Yard for their financial
support in 2017 that enabled us to undertake a large conservation
project to conserve art works, furniture and furnishings.

Design by A Practice for Everyday Life
Printed by Graphius, Belgium
Photography by Paul Allitt and Ed Park

ISBN 978-1-904561-75-0
Edition of 7,500; 2018 edition, third printing

Kettle's Yard
Castle Street, Cambridge CB3 0AQ
United Kingdom
+44 (0)1223 748 100
kettlesyard.co.uk

Director: Andrew Nairne OBE
Chair: Dr Rowan Williams

Front cover: View of the sitting room
Inside front cover: View of the downstairs extension
Inside back cover: View of the extension showing works by Italo Valenti

Support
Join a growing group of supporters enabling us to undertake
new research, make outstanding exhibitions, work with schools,
young people and the community, and conserve the Kettle's Yard
House and collection for future generations.

Find out how you can help and become involved:
kettlesyard.co.uk/support or call +44 (0)1223 748 100